BAZOOKA BOYS!

Be Strong & Be Brave...
for the Lord your God is with you.
Deuteronomy 31:6

By
Kristie Kerr & Paula Yarnes
with
Jeff Kerr & Alan Bach

CONTENTS

What is Self-Control 1-20
   Lesson 2
   Doodle Page 9
   Activity Sheet 11
   Bazooka Breakdown 15
   Bazooka Project 19

Good Fruit / Bad Fruit 21-34
   Lesson 22
   Doodle Page .28
   Activity Sheet 29
   Bazooka Breakdown 32
   Bazooka Project 34

Mind Control 35-52
   Lesson 36
   Doodle Page .42
   Activity Sheet 43
   Bazooka Breakdown 48
   Bazooka Project 51

Watch Your Mouth 53-66
   Lesson 54
   Doodle Page .60
   Activity Sheet 61
   Bazooka Breakdown 64
   Bazooka Project 66

Money Matters 67-78
   Lesson 68
   Doodle Page .72
   Activity Sheet 73
   Bazooka Breakdown 75
   Bazooka Project 77

Using My Gifts 79-98
   Lesson 80
   Doodle Page .88
   Activity Sheet 89
   Bazooka Breakdown 92
   Bazooka Project 94

Taking My Time 99-114
   Lesson 100
   Doodle Page 107
   Activity Sheet 108
   Bazooka Breakdown 112
   Bazooka Project 114

The Way to Obey 115-130
   Lesson 116
   Doodle Page 122
   Activity Sheet 123
   Bazooka Breakdown 127
   Bazooka Project 129

Your Body, God's House 131-142
   Lesson 132
   Doodle Page 136
   Activity Sheet 137
   Bazooka Breakdown 141
   Bazooka Project 142

Hands and Feet 143-157
   Lesson 144
   Doodle Page 148
   Activity Sheet 149
   Bazooka Breakdown 154
   Bazooka Project 157

Dedicated to the boys who inspire us:

To Charlie whose tender heart and quiet spirit
remind us that **STRENGTH ISN'T ALWAYS LOUD**.

To Hunter who is **TENACIOUS AND KIND**...
and came up with the name Bazooka Boys.

To Chase who **LOVES UNCONDITIONALLY**.

To Reed who lit his homework on fire...
and then became an **HONOR STUDENT**.

To Jacob, the boy with the sensitive heart,
that captures people with his **LOVE FOR JUSTICE AND ALL THINGS SILLY**.

To Levi whose **DETERMINATION COULD DEMOLISH MOUNTAINS**
& smile could melt away the debris

To Zach who is a **TRUSTWORTHY, CONFIDENT, KIND-HEARTED** young man,
and NEVER forgets to kiss his mom goodnight!

To Li who is **KIND AND LOVING** and **ALWAYS** follows the rules!

To Stewart. The **TWINKLE IN YOUR EYE** and the tenderness in your heart
remind us that God really does make dreams come true.

You amaze us.
Go change the world.

Bazooka Boys ★ Who Am I?

SELF-CONTROL

WEEK 1

WHAT IS SELF-CONTROL?

WHAT'S THE POINT?
GOD WANTS TO HELP ME CONTROL MYSELF.

THEME VERSE:
So think clearly and exercise self-control.
1 Peter 1:13

RELATED BIBLE PASSAGE:
Romans 7:15–25

When I was young, I would make the same New Year's resolution every single year without fail. I would sit in my room on December 31 and decide—with everything in my being—that this would be the year that I would reach my goal. I would be victorious! I would be a conqueror! I would do it!

What was this amazing goal, you ask?

Well, every year, I would resolve that I would not do anything wrong for an entire year.

Yup, you heard me right. No talking back to my parents. No sneaking a cookie after my mom told me I couldn't have one. No fighting with my sister. No talking in class when I wasn't supposed to. No getting into trouble.

You can imagine how far I got into the year before I blew it. Usually until about 9:38 a.m. on January 1. If I lasted even that long.

I would get so disappointed in myself. Why couldn't I do it? Why couldn't I stay out of trouble for at least one measly little day? In my heart, I so desperately wanted to do the right thing all the time, but I found that something inside of me always seemed to take over and I found myself making a bad choice once again.

Have you ever had that happen to you? You know that you shouldn't disobey your parents…you actually really want to honor your mom and dad, yet you find yourself doing the very thing they told you not to do.

Maybe you promise yourself that you're going to stop talking about your friends when they're not around, but then all your other friends start gossiping and you find yourself going along with what everyone else is doing. You leave the conversation wondering, how did that happen!? I was so sure I was going to do better this time!

Or maybe you're really trying to not put off your homework so much. You come home from school determined to get your work done right away. But then you turn on the TV or

Bazooka Boys ★ Who Am I?

start playing on the computer. Before you know it, your mom is upset with you once again because you forgot to get your homework done. Again.

Why does this happen? How can we be SO determined to do the right thing, and then find ourselves failing over and over again?

I asked God this question a few years ago. I was really frustrated with myself because no matter how hard I tried, I kept stumbling into the same mistakes over and over again. I really wanted to do the right thing, but something inside of me seemed to fight against it.

And God began to show me that I was making these same mistakes because I wasn't practicing self-control.

SELF-CONTROL... MEANS... WELL... CONTROLLING YOURSELF!

It means **MAKING** yourself do the right thing at the right time.

I think a lot of you are like me. A lot of my areas of weakness and frustration are directly linked to the fact that I don't control myself. I know the right thing, but I don't do it. I pause and say, "Oh, I shouldn't," but then I go ahead and do it anyway. Or even worse, I don't even realize I'm not practicing self-control! I just don't pay attention. I'm acting without thinking. I'm not stopping to make sure I make good choices.

That—I am beginning to realize—is a dangerous road to be on. These might seem like small little things, but let's be honest: if we cannot control ourselves in the small things, why do we think we can control ourselves in the big things?

I recently read an article about a woman who made a really bad choice that caused a lot of people a whole lot of pain. She said, "I never once thought what I was doing was okay, but I just didn't want to stop."

Wow. Knowing what we should do and not doing it. Facing the choices of right and wrong and not having the self-control to choose the right thing even when your heart and body and mind are telling you to do the wrong thing. This "self-control" stuff is a big, big deal.

> "FOR I WAS BORN A SINNER."
> —PSALM 51:5

I had a friend who used to say, "Sin is saying, 'I'm going to have what I want, when I want it.'" You may have never thought about disobeying your parents as sin, but that's exactly what it is. Sin. Saying, "I know that I shouldn't do this, but I'm going to do it anyway"—no matter how big or how small the issue may be—is a sure sign of a sinful heart.

The Bible tells us we're all born with a sinful nature. There's something inside of us that doesn't want to do the right thing! King David wrote in Psalm 51:5, "*For I was born a sinner*". You don't have to teach a two-year-old to hit his friend upside the head when he wants to take his toy—it comes naturally because he has a sinful nature, just like the rest of us.

EVEN THOUGH YOU AND I WANT TO DO THE RIGHT THING, THERE ALWAYS SEEMS TO BE SOMETHING PULLING AT US THAT MAKES US WANT TO DO THE WRONG THING INSTEAD.

Paul talks about this very thing in Romans 7:

> *"And I know that nothing good lives in me, that is, in my sinful nature. I want to do what is right, but I can't. I want to do what is good, but I don't. I don't want to do what is wrong, but I do it anyway* (vs. 18–19)."

Bazooka Boys ★ Who Am I?

Can anyone relate to our buddy, Paul? He's describing in detail what it means to not have self-control. Deep in his heart, he wants to do the right things, but he feels the war within him. The things he wants to do, he doesn't do. And the things he doesn't want to do, he finds himself doing. Let's keep reading…

"But if I do what I don't want to do, I am not really the one doing wrong; it is sin living in me that does it. I have discovered this principle of life—that when I want to do what is right, I inevitably do what is wrong (vs. 20–21)."

Paul is telling us that no matter how hard we really want to do the right thing, the sinful nature inside of us will always be fighting against us. Now does this mean that whenever you do something wrong, you can simply say, "Sorry Mom, my sinful nature made me do it"? You can give it a try, but I don't think she's going to buy it!

BUT, it can still be helpful to realize that there's really something going on inside us that makes it hard to do the right thing.

I used to get pretty discouraged and upset with myself when I couldn't make my New Year's Resolution happen. I would beat myself up and wonder what was wrong with me. Paul shows this same frustration in Romans 7 when he says, *"Oh what a miserable person I am! Who will free me from this life that is dominated by sin and death?* (vs. 24)."

So what are we to do about this? How can we learn to do the right thing at the right time? How do we learn the art of self-control?

 1. ASK GOD TO HELP.

If you were to read a book on self-control, you would find a lot of talk about willpower and motivation and working really hard to meet your goal. I'm not saying those things are bad—you're definitely going to need a healthy dose of each of those things in order to live a self-controlled life. But if we believe what Paul is saying in Romans, then we should realize that not having self-control is a spiritual problem. There's sin at work in our hearts, which causes us to struggle with doing the right thing.

BOTTOM LINE: YOU CAN'T DO IT BY YOURSELF.

Without Jesus, we're powerless against sin. Our sinful nature is strong, and there's only one thing stronger: Jesus.

Romans 7:24–25 says, *"Who will free me from this life that is dominated by sin and death? Thank God! The answer is in Jesus Christ our Lord."*

Yes, your sinful nature is strong. But Jesus is stronger! Yes, it can be hard to fight to do the right thing. But Jesus has promised to help you!

When we ask Jesus to come into our lives, He comes and lives inside of us and helps us do the right thing. He has broken the power of sin in us, and if we choose to let Him, He will give us the strength to do the right thing. His Holy Spirit fills us with power, and we're suddenly able to conquer those areas of our lives that we used to think would always beat us. Jesus is stronger than our sinful nature.

As we talk about self-control in this Bible study, I know there will be times where you feel discouraged and think you just have to **tRY** harder. I want to encourage you, in those moments when you feel weak, remember that Jesus is the source of your strength! Ask Him to help you and believe that He will help you control yourself.

 2. tRAIN YOURSELF tO BE DISCIPLINED.

First Corinthians 9:27 says, *"I discipline my body like an athlete, training it to do what it should."*

Calvin loves to play soccer. He's been playing since he was really little, and every year he gets better and better. But this year, he has a new coach who's pushing him harder than anyone ever has before. During practice, he makes the team do drills over and over again. They would practice kicking the ball back and forth, back and forth over and over and over again until Calvin wanted to scream.

Finally, one day he asked his coach, "Why do we practice the same drill so much?" He said, "We practice over and over again because during the game, it's so easy to become distracted by the crowd, the other team, and even your own emotions. When you practice the same drill over and over again, your mind will automatically know what to do in the heat of the moment because you have trained yourself. It prepares you for the moment of truth when you need to rely on what you've learned, even when it's challenging."

It's the same way with **EVERYTHING** in life! The more you practice, the easier it is to remember what you're supposed to do. The more you practice your math flashcards, the easier it is to remember your math facts. The more you practice your piano lesson, the easier it is for you to play through the songs you're learning. The more you practice riding that new skateboard, the less likely you are to fall on your booty!

Training ourselves to be self-controlled is so important. That means that we have to make ourselves do the right thing even when we don't feel like it. We choose to get up off the couch and help our mom with the dishes the first time she asks us. We pick the apple off the snack cart even though we **REALLY** want the cookie because we know the apple is better for us. We tell our sinful nature **"NO"** and control ourselves!

You know why it's so important to train yourself to be self-controlled in the everyday things?

KA-BOOM!!!!

Because the self-control I use when I help my mom with the dishes is the same self-control I use when I say "no" to the friend asking me to cheat on a test. The self-control I use when I pick an apple is the same self-control I use when I don't steal that video game I really, really want but can't afford. The self-control that makes us choose the right thing with the little stuff is the same self-control that will help us choose the right thing with the big stuff.

1 Timothy 4:8 says, "*Physical training is good, but training for godliness is much better, promising benefits in this life and in the life to come.*" I love how the Message version translates this same verse: "*Exercise daily in God—no spiritual flabbiness, please! Workouts in the gymnasium are useful, but a disciplined life in God is far more so, making you fit both today and forever.*"

You need to train yourself to be self-controlled. Do something to work toward discipline. Practice saying "no" to your sinful nature. Challenge yourself in the small things so you will know how to discipline yourself in the big things.

The bottom line is this: Self-control is simply listening to what God tells you to do—and then doing it.

PRETTY SIMPLE, RIGHT?

Well, it may be simple, but simple doesn't necessarily mean easy. Let's trust God to help us be disciplined and self-controlled in every area of our lives. Jesus has promised to help us, so let's do it!

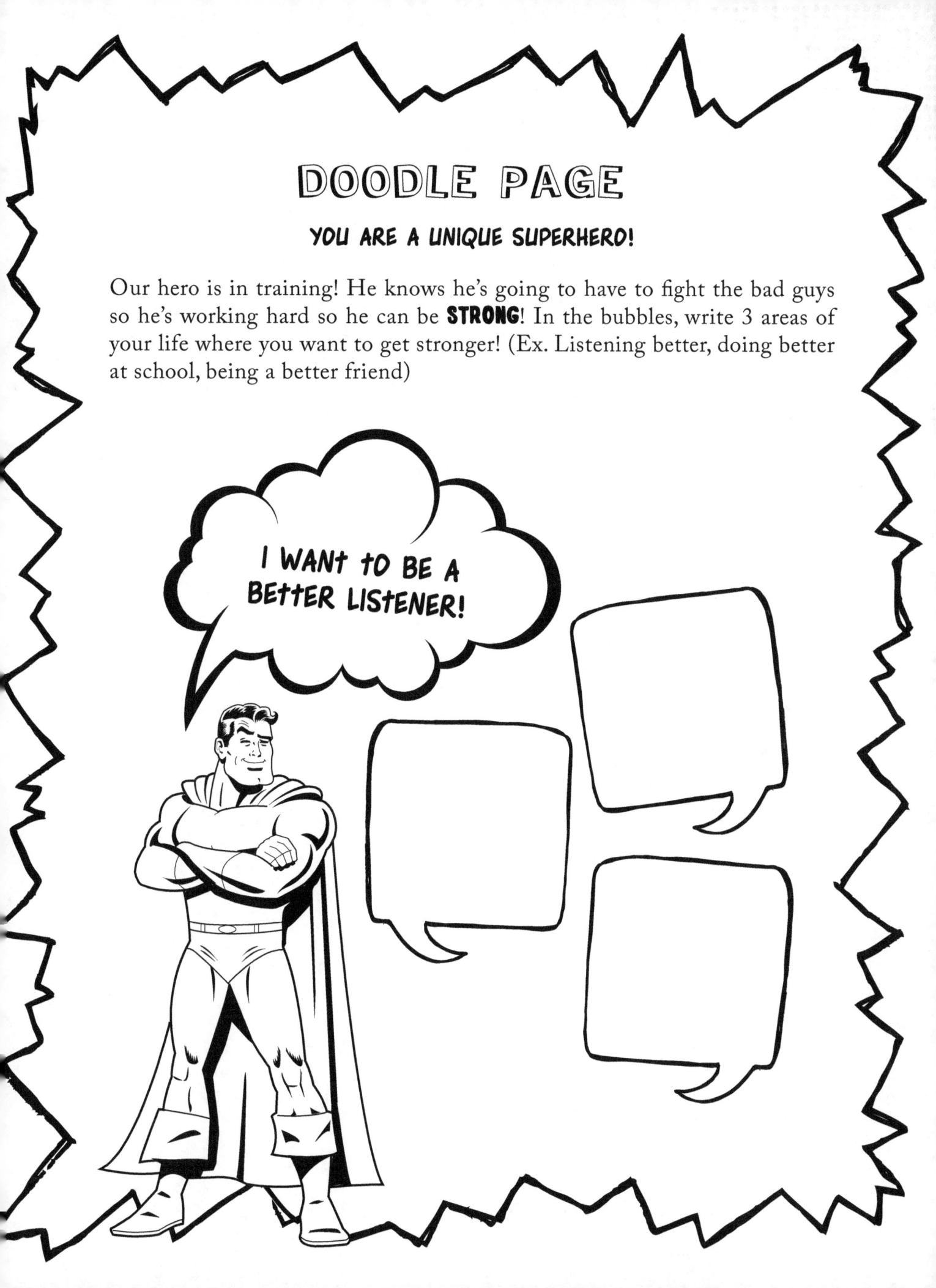

Bazooka Boys ★ Who Am I?

WEEK 1

God wants to help you control yourself.

One of the ways God wants you to grow in self-control is by spending time praying and reading the Bible every day.

Draw a picture of yourself reading the Bible.

DRAW IT HERE!!!

In Romans 7, Paul talks about wanting to do the right thing, but something inside of him pulls at him to do the wrong thing instead. Jesus wants us to have self-control. It's much better to think before you act.

Find your way through the maze. Remember to think before you act!

Bazooka Boys ★ Who Am I?

You need to train yourself to be self-controlled. Next to each letter, list something you can do to work toward self-discipline. **Remember:** Challenge yourself in the small things so you will know how to discipline yourself in the big things.

Example: S - Scripture memorization

S _____

E _____

L _____

F _____

C _____

O _____

N _____

T _____

R _____

O _____

L _____

In Romans 7, Paul describes in detail what it means to not have self-control. Deep in his heart, he wants to do the right things, but he feels the war within himself. The things he wants to do, he doesn't do. And the things he *doesn't* want to do, he finds himself doing.

Read Romans 7:15–25 in your Bible, and fill in the missing words in the verses below (all verses NIV).

v. 15 *I do not _____ what I do. For what I want to do I do not do, but what I hate I do.*

v. 16 *And if I do what I do not _____ to do, I agree that the law is good.*

v. 17 *As it is, it is no longer I myself who do it, but it is _____ living in me.*

v. 18 *For I know that _____ itself does not dwell in me, that is, in my sinful nature. For I have the desire to do what is good, but I cannot carry it out.*

v. 19 *For I do not do the good I want to do, but the _____ I do not want to do—this I keep on doing.*

v. 20 *Now if I do what I do not want to do, it is no longer I who do it, but it is sin _____ in me that does it.*

v. 21 *I find this _____ at work: Although I want to do good, evil is right there with me.*

v. 22 *For in my inner being I delight in _____ law;*

v. 23 *But I see another law at work in me, waging war against the law of my mind and making me a _____ of the law of sin at work within me.*

v. 24 *What a wretched man I am! Who will _____ me from this body that is subject to death?*

v. 25 *Thanks be to God, who _____ me through Jesus Christ our Lord! So then, I myself in my mind am a slave to God's law, but in my sinful nature a slave to the law of sin.*

Word List

Understand	Living	Evil	God's
Law	Sin	Delivers	Save
Good	Prisoner	Want	

Bazooka Boys ★ Who Am I?

BAZOOKA BREAKDOWN

Have you ever decided you were **NEVER** going to do something again, and yet did it anyway? Or maybe there is something you decided you were **GOING** to do every day like practicing your piano or being nice to your brother, and yet you found yourself **NOT** doing that thing?

In the space provided, write out what you it was—or draw a picture.

In Romans 7, Paul talks about wanting to do the right thing, but something inside of him pulls at him to do the wrong thing instead. It's like a tug of war between doing the right thing and doing the wrong thing! Do you remember what Paul said is pulling at him? Write it in the space on the left side of the rope.

Romans 7 also tells us that only one thing is stronger than our sinful nature? Do you remember what that is? Write your answer on the right side of the rope!

Bazooka Boys ★ Who Am I?

WEEK 1

God wants us to train ourselves to be more self-controlled. Below, five different situations are listed. In the spaces provided, write out 5 things you could do to practice self-control in each situation.

- My mom asks me to pick up my coat
- I'm really mad at my sister and want to yell at her
- I want to eat a bag of candy even though its almost dinnertime
- I want to talk to my friend while the teacher is talking
- I have spent an hour playing video games

Bazooka Boys ★ Who Am I?

PRAYERCHUTES

This project is especially fun if you can get to a balcony level to launch your prayerchutes. If not, simply throw your prayerchutes into the air!

Supplies

- Cone shape coffee filter
- Army figurine
- 2 Strings (about one foot long)
- Clear tape
- Crayons and markers

Prep

- In black marker, write verse "*So think clearly and exercise self-control.*" on the coffee filter.

Directions

- Color the coffee filter.
- Open up the coffee filter and tie one end of each string to the army figurine, taping the other end to the inside of the coffee filter.
- Throw your prayerchute into the air and watch it fly!

Bazooka Boys ★ Who Am I?

GOOD FRUIT / BAD FRUIT

What's the Point?
I need to push down my flesh and fill up with the Holy Spirit!

THEME VERSE:

*So I say, let the Holy Spirit guide your lives.
Then you won't be doing what your sinful nature craves.*
Galatians 5:16

RELATED BIBLE PASSAGE:

Galatians 5:16–26

"I hate cleaning my room!"

Joseph was stomping around his room, throwing things into his closet and muttering under his breath. All his friends were outside enjoying the sunshine while he sat indoors picking up clothes off the floor.

"It's not fair," he said to himself. "All my friends get to do whatever they want. Why does my mom always make me do what **SHE** wants me to do? I just want to be able to do what I want to do!"

Have you ever had that happen to you? You **REALLY** want to play outside with your friends, but your parents make you do chores first? Or you **REALLY** want to have free time in class, but your teacher makes you do an extra assignment first? Or maybe you really want to play a certain game, but it's your friend's turn to choose and you have to play what he wants instead?

We can probably all remember a time when we didn't get what we wanted. It can be pretty frustrating.

Imagine what it would be like if you could do whatever you wanted **ALL** the time! Chocolate ice cream for breakfast, lunch, and dinner. Recess for four hours a day. No homework. No chores. As much TV and computer time as you want – whenever you want it.

Sounds pretty good, doesn't it?

Bazooka Boys ★ Who Am I?

ZAP!!! Well, it does sound good at first, but what happens when your stomach hurts and you get a toothache from only eating chocolate ice cream? And what happens when you grow up and you don't know how to read or do math because you had recess all day at school instead of learning the things you needed to learn? And what happens when you **NEVER** clean your room and suddenly you can't find any clean clothes to wear to school and your room starts to smell really bad because of all the stinky socks stuck in the corner? That doesn't sound like much fun either.

Sometimes we think of freedom as being able to do whatever we want. We think we should only have to do the things that are fun! We think we should be able to do things whenever we want to—instead of when our teacher or parents want us to do things. We try and avoid things that are hard and not so fun. But that isn't the way life works. Most of life is made up of doing the things that we **SHOULD** do, not the things we **WANT** to do.

You may not feel like cleaning your room, but you know it's the right thing to do. You may not feel like doing your homework, but you do it because you know it's important to learn things. You may not feel like taking turns with your friends, but you do it because you know a good friend takes turns.

ONE OF THE GREATEST WAYS THAT WE CAN PRACTICE SELF-CONTROL IS BY DOING THE THINGS WE MAY NOT WANT TO DO, BUT THEY'RE THE RIGHT THINGS TO DO.

Joseph didn't **WANT** to pick up his room, but when he choose to obey his parents and do what they asked, he was choosing what was better. He was showing honor to his parents. He was being responsible by taking care of the things he owned. He was being a good example to his friends by doing the right thing. More important than all these things, something happened inside Joseph when he decided to do the right thing, even when he didn't feel like it.

You see, something happens in us when we put aside our own feelings and do what we **SHOULD** do, even when we don't **WANT** to.

The Bible talks a lot about our **FLESH**. What in the world does "flesh" mean? Well, it's the thing inside of us that makes us only think about ourselves and what we want. It's part of the "sinful nature" we talked about last week. It's the little voice inside your head that says, "You should always get what you want." It whispers, "You shouldn't have to do anything you don't want to do." The flesh is all about me, me, me. Making ME happy. Making sure I always get to do what I want.

Ick. Our flesh is pretty yucky.

Jesus tells us over and over again that we should not let our flesh be the boss of us. We should think of others before ourselves. We should do the right thing even if it's not easy. Our flesh wants to lead us down one path, but God's path is way better!

So, how do we fight this flesh thing? How do we overcome that voice that tells us to only do what we want instead of what's right?

There's a magic formula! Ready?

 We **PUSH** down the **FLESH** and **FILL UP** with the **SPIRIT**!

 1. PUSH DOWN OUR FLESH.

Galatians 5:16 says, *"So I say, let the Holy Spirit guide your lives. Then you won't be doing what your sinful nature craves."*

Remember last week when we talked about the two sides pulling at us? The tug of war to do the right thing verses the tug of war to do the wrong thing? That's what this verse is talking about. Good and evil are at WAR inside us!

We have to **FIGHT** hard to help the good side win. And the more the good side wins, the stronger it becomes.

Having self-control means you push down your flesh with everything in you. You tell your mind and body and actions "**NO!**"

When your flesh tells you to take that cookie even though your Mom told you not to, you push down your flesh and say, "**NO COOKIE FOR YOU!**" When your flesh tells you to share that secret about a friend that you promised you wouldn't share, you push down your flesh and say, "**NO! I'M NOT GOING TO TELL THAT SECRET!**" When your flesh tells you to cheat on the test so you can get a better grade, you push down your flesh and say, "**NO! I'M NOT GOING TO DO SOMETHING I KNOW IS WRONG!**"

First Corinthians 9:27 says, "*I keep my body under control and make it my slave …*"(CEV). Another version says, "*It is my own body I fight to make it do what I want*" (ERV). Sometimes the thing we're fighting is our very own body. Sometimes I have to smack myself upside the head and say, "No! I will not listen to you! I will not let you be the boss of me!"

Push down your flesh. Don't let it bully you into doing something you know is wrong.

So, we push down then flesh, and then we…

 ## 2. FILL UP WITH THE SPIRIT.

Micah 3:8 says, "*But me—I'm filled with God's power…*" (MSG). And Acts 1:8 says, "*But you will receive power when the Holy Spirit comes upon you*".

When you push down that gross, yucky flesh, you make room for God's awesome and amazing power to fill you up! The Holy Spirit gives you the **POWER** to fight your flesh and have self-control!

Austin was feeling super nervous about going to school. Every morning he would begin walking toward his school and his mind would start picturing every possible bad thing that could ever happen. He worried that he would drop his tray at lunch. He wondered if his teacher would call on him when he didn't know the answer. He thought about how embarrassed he would be if he didn't have anyone to play with at recess. The more he thought about it, the more anxious and afraid he would get. His thoughts kept coming faster and faster until his heart was beating fast and he thought he might throw up.

But he remembered that he didn't have to let his thoughts boss him around, so the next time a bad thought came into his head, he pushed down his flesh and told it to go away. Over and over again, he knocked those thoughts right out of his head and told them to go away.

Austin realized that, not only did he need to get the bad thoughts out, he needed to fill up with good thoughts. He asked the Holy Spirit to come and fill his thoughts with good things instead. He prayed for the Holy Spirit's power to give him strength to fight his flesh. He remembered a verse his mom taught him that said, *"For I can do everything through Christ who gives me strength"* (Philippians 4:13), and he started saying it over and over again.

He pushed those bad thoughts out and filled his mind with the power of the Holy Spirit. Every time he pushed down the flesh, he filled the space with a reminder that God was with him and he could do anything with God's help!

The Holy Spirit will fill you with the power to overcome your flesh. He will fight it for you. When you ask Him to help you, His strength comes into you and gives you **SUPERNATURAL** power to practice self-control.

So, we push down our flesh, we fill up with the Spirit, and then we . . .

 ## 3. GROW SOME FRUIT.

What kind of tree grows an apple? What kind of tree grows an orange? What kind of tree grows a lemon?

Of course an apple tree grows apples. An orange tree grows oranges. And a lemon tree grows lemons. You can tell what kind of tree it is by the kind of fruit it produces. It even says this in the Bible. Luke 6:44 says, *"A tree is identified by its fruit."*

It's the same way with our lives. The Bible says that if we really love Jesus and we're following Him, we'll see certain kinds of fruit in our lives. Galatians 5:22 says, *"But the Holy Spirit produces this kind of fruit in our lives: love, joy, peace, patience, kindness, goodness, faithfulness, gentleness, and self-control."*

If our lives belong to Jesus, the "fruit" of our lives—the things other people notice about us—should be love, joy, peace, and all the other fruits of the Spirit...including self-control!

If we push down our flesh and we fill up with the Spirit, then we'll see more and more of these things in our lives. If I'm filling myself with the Spirit, I'll be a more loving person. If I'm filling myself with the Spirit, I'll be a more patient person. If I'm filling myself with the Spirit, I'll have more self-control.

The reverse is also true, isn't it? If you're not very loving, you need more of the Spirit. If you're not very patient, you need more of the Spirit. And if your life isn't demonstrating self-control, you need more of the Spirit.

If our fruit shows a lack of peace, we need less of the flesh and more of the Spirit. If our fruit shows a lack of gentleness—we're harsh and snappy and unkind—we need less of our flesh and more of the Spirit. And if we find ourselves struggling to be disciplined, we need less of the flesh and more of the Spirit.

What is the secret to discipline? Less of the flesh and more, more, more of Jesus.

He is the answer. He is where we go to deal with our lack of discipline.

PUSH DOWN THE FLESH, FILL UP WITH MORE OF THE SPIRIT, AND GROW GOOD FRUIT.

DOODLE PAGE

LESSON 2

In each of the fruits below, write one way you could have the fruit of the spirit more evident in your life this week.

ACTIVITY SHEET

WEEK 2

Galatians 5:22–23 tells us that the fruit of the Spirit is: love, joy, peace, patience, kindness, goodness, faithfulness, gentleness, and self-control.

Write out the name of each fruit on the tree and then color in the picture!

Look up Galatians 5 in your Bible. Verses 19–21 list 16 bad things that will show up in your life if you're letting your flesh control you. What are they?

1.
2.
3.
4.
5.
6.
7.
8.
9.
10.
11.
12.
13.
14.
15.
16.

Bazooka Boys ★ Who Am I?

WEEK 2

Verse 22 tells us the good fruit that will be present in a life that is controlled by the Spirit. List those nine things here:

1.

2.

3.

4.

5.

6.

7.

8.

9.

BAZOOKA BREAKDOWN

Our flesh is the part of us that wants whatever it wants whenever it wants it. We push down our flesh when we tell our bodies who's boss, we tell ourselves **NO**, and we do what is right even if we don't want to. Draw a picture of yourself in the space provided and remind yourself that your body doesn't get to boss you around!

Bazooka Boys ★ Who Am I?

After we push down the flesh, what do we do?

We _____ up with the _____!

Look up Galatians 5:22 in your Bible and copy the verse in the space provided.

Look at the fruit listed in the verse above. What kind of fruit do you think is showing the MOST in your life? What kind of fruit is showing LEAST in your life? Write it in the space below.

HOLY SPIRIT BALLOON EXPERIMENT

(*This is a fun project! DO NOT do this without parental supervision!)

Supplies
- Balloon
- One candle
- Lighter or match

Prep
- Fill one balloon with water.

Directions

1. Blow up the balloon.
2. Option: Draw a face on the balloon with a sharpie.
3. Set up candle on table.
4. Have a grown-up take the balloons and put them over the flame. The flame will pop the balloons.
5. Place the water balloon over the flame to demonstrate that a balloon filled with water will not pop.

The balloon full of air represents our flesh or our selfishness. It is full of our own air, leaving no room for the Holy Spirit.

And just like the balloon full of air pops when it gets next to the flame, we will fall apart when we face temptation if we are full our flesh.

But the balloon filled with water represents the Holy Spirit! If we are full of the Holy Spirit, we have the power to resist temptation. The water balloon over the flame does not burn or pop. And if we fill ourselves up with the Holy Spirit, we will stay strong no matter what we face!

Bazooka Boys ★ Who Am I?

MIND CONTROL

WHAT'S THE POINT?
GOD WANTS YOU TO THINK ABOUT GOOD THINGS, NOT BAD THINGS!

THEME VERSE:
Fix your thoughts on what is true, and honorable, and right, and pure, and lovely, and admirable. Think about things that are excellent and worthy of praise.
Philippians 4:8

RELATED BIBLE PASSAGE:
Romans 8

Our brains are pretty amazing things. Some people say the average human thinks 70,000 thoughts every single day. That's a lot of thinking!

The Bible tells us Jesus knows **EVERY SINGLE THOUGHT WE HAVE!** Psalm 94:11 says, *"The Lord knows people's thoughts."* I'm not sure how I feel about that. On one hand, it's so incredible to know God understands every single thing about me without me even saying a word, but on the other hand, I wouldn't say I'm totally proud of each and every thought that crosses my mind. I'm usually happy when I don't act on a negative thought, but the Bible says that if I even think it, He knows it. Yikes! Even more reason to be amazed at God's love for me—He knows everything I think about and still loves me. Crazy!

The Bible encourages us to be careful about the things we think about. God knows how easy it is to think about things we shouldn't. We all have areas of our lives where we allow our thoughts to go places they shouldn't. And sometimes we find our train of thought stuck on a certain pattern of behavior or consumed by a certain way of thinking.

Some of us get stuck always thinking negative thoughts. We can be critical of other people—always putting them down in our minds. We can also be critical of ourselves—saying negative things to ourselves all the time like, "You're so dumb! No one likes you! You're not good at anything!" God doesn't want us to always think negative thoughts.

Maybe you've seen something you shouldn't have seen or done something you shouldn't have done, and now you can't stop thinking about something you know isn't honoring to God.

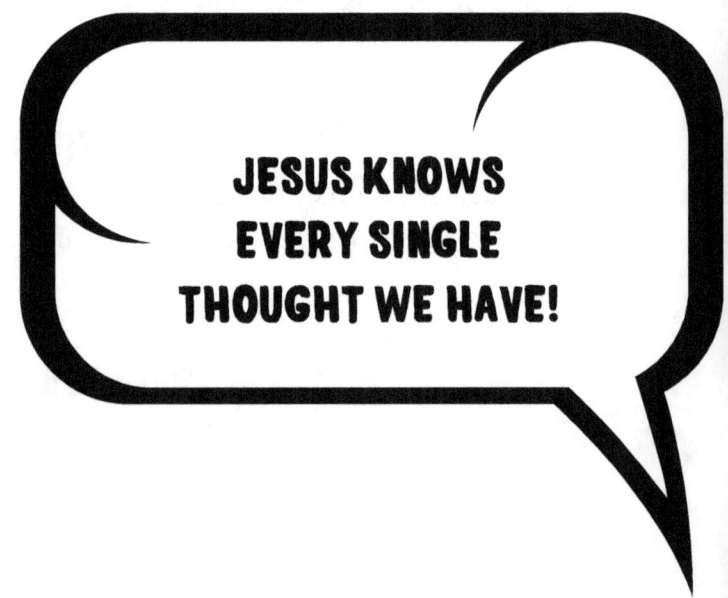

Some of us get stuck thinking about the past. You can't help but remember and think about things that happened in the past. Maybe you keep thinking about a mistake you made and you replay it over and over again in your mind. It can be so easy to get stuck in the past.

Bazooka Boys ★ Who Am I?

Maybe your mind gets stuck in WORRY mode and your thoughts are consumed by what COULD happen. Your thoughts might even be kind of scary. Your mind seems to always think about the worst possible thing, and you have a hard time stopping it.

So, I have a question for you: why do we let our thoughts focus on such negative things?

Maybe that seems like a trick question. You might be thinking, "What do you mean I 'let' my thoughts be negative?" I don't know about you, but many times I think I don't have any control over the thoughts going through my head. They seem to just happen!

But God tells us that we should CONTROL the thoughts going through our mind. What does it mean to control something? It means you're the BOSS of it. You're in charge and it has to do whatever you tell it to do.

Remember last week when we talked about 1 Corinthians 9:27? It says, "*I keep my body under control and make it my slave...*"(CEV). Well, the most important part of your body to keep as your slave is your BRAIN. You can't just let your thoughts go wherever they want to go. Make them your slaves and tell them they have to do whatever you tell them to do!

YOU KNOW WHY THAT'S SO IMPORTANT? BECAUSE YOUR THOUGHTS EVENTUALLY BECOME YOUR ACTIONS.

You might think it's not harming anyone else to think bad things, but the truth is that whatever you're thinking about eventually comes out in the way you treat others. Most of all, it will hurt YOU. Proverbs 4:23 says, "*Above all, be careful what you think because your thoughts control your life*" (ERV). The things you think about are important.

Last week, we talked about the fruit of the Spirit: love, joy, peace, patience, kindness, goodness, faithfulness, gentleness, and self-control. This is the good fruit that should be overflowing in our lives. But you know what? Your mind is an easy place to grow **BAD** fruit.

We aren't very loving because we're filled with unloving thoughts toward other people. We're not filled with joy because our minds are focused on disappointments. Our minds aren't peaceful because we're worried about so many things. We're not patient, kind, good, faithful, or gentle in our thoughts. Instead, we're impatient, rude, harsh, disloyal, and destructive in the things we think about.

So, how can we learn to discipline our thoughts?

 ## 1. LET THE HOLY SPIRIT BE THE BOSS OF YOUR BRAIN!

Who gets to be the boss of your brain? The Holy Spirit! Romans 8:6 says, "*So letting your sinful nature control your mind leads to death. But letting the Spirit control your mind leads to life and peace.*"

We need to push down the flesh that wants to fill our thoughts with negative and sinful things, and instead fill up our minds with the Holy Spirit. Invite the Holy Spirit into your thoughts. Say, "Holy Spirit, you're the boss of my brain!" When He's in charge, He will fill up your mind with all the good fruit of the Spirit and there won't be room for all that yucky, negative stuff!

Bazooka Boys ★ Who Am I?

The second way you can discipline your THOUGHTS is to…

 2. KICK THE HABIT!

What's a habit? It's something you do all the time without thinking about it. Some people have a habit of biting their nails or chewing with their mouth open. What habits to you have?

We all have habits—and it's no different when it comes to our thought life. It's easy to get in the habit of thinking in a certain way or constantly focusing on a certain topic. And if you want to break **ANY** habit, you have to work hard at changing your behavior. You have to **KICK THE HABIT**!

If you're in the habit of thinking of the worst things all the time, you're going to need to change that behavior. Catch yourself focusing on bad stuff. When you realize you're thinking something that isn't good, stop yourself right away and begin to think about good things instead!

Landon had a hard time falling asleep. Every night he would crawl into bed and his mind would begin to go crazy. He would imagine all kinds of scary things.

He would imagine there was something in his closet. He would imagine he was lost and couldn't find his mom. Sometimes he even imagined missing the goal in the final seconds of a championship hockey game and letting all his teammates down! He wasn't sure where all these negative thoughts came from, but they sure did bother him.

One day he realized he had gotten in the habit of thinking bad things every night at bedtime. It just got to be the way his brain decided to boss him around at night. So he decided to **KICK tHE HABIt**!

When he got into bed, as soon as the first scary thought popped into his mind, he thought of something funny instead. Or he would repeat a Bible verse his mom had taught him: *"Be strong and courageous! Do not be afraid, for the Lord God is with you wherever you go"* (Joshua 1:9). Every time his brain tried to take him back to a scary thought, he **KICKED** that habit right in the teeth and thought of something GOOD instead.

You are in control of what you think about. You have the power to simply stop thinking about things that make you sad, worried, or frustrated. Refuse to focus on those things. Kick that bad habit, and think about good stuff instead! Don't allow your thoughts to go wherever they want to. You can control what you think about.

Psalm 119:95 says, *"…I will quietly keep my mind on Your laws."* You have the power to keep your mind fixed on the things you want to think about, like what God says is true. And you have the power to keep your mind away from the things you shouldn't be thinking about.

And the last way you can discipline your thoughts is to focus on…

3. tHE "W" PLAN!

One of my all-time favorite verses in the Bible is Philippians 4:8: *"Finally, brothers and sisters, whatever is true, whatever is noble, whatever is right, whatever is pure, whatever is lovely, whatever is admirable—if anything is excellent or praiseworthy—think about such things."*

Isn't that a great verse? It tells us to think about **"WHATEVER"** is good! And **"WHATEVER** is true! And **"WHATEVER"** is lovely! So when I'm having a hard time controlling my thoughts, I put up three fingers to make a "W" and start using my "W" plan!

What is the "W" plan?

Well, when a thought comes knocking at the door to my brain, I pretend there's a little peep-hole to look through the door and before I answer it I say, "Are you a **WHATEVER** thought?" I'm basically asking, "Are you a good thought or a bad thought?" and "Are you a true thought or a lie?" and "Are you a lovely thought or a scary thought?" If it's not a "WHATEVER" thought, I don't open the door! I tell those yucky thoughts to stay outside my brain. I don't want them in there!

Now, we all have times when a bad thought sneaks into our brain. It's just part of being human. But we can decide how long we let those thoughts stick around.

You don't have to **LET** just any thought just roam around in your brain. If you let the Holy Spirit be the boss, He will help you think about love, joy, peace, and other good things! He will help you **KICK THE HABIT** of thinking about things that aren't good for you.

Colossians 3:2 says, *"Set your mind on things above, not things of earth"* (NIV). God wants your mind to be a place with lots of good fruit. He doesn't want you feeling sad, scared, angry, or negative all the time. Choose to make your brain a place full of good stuff!

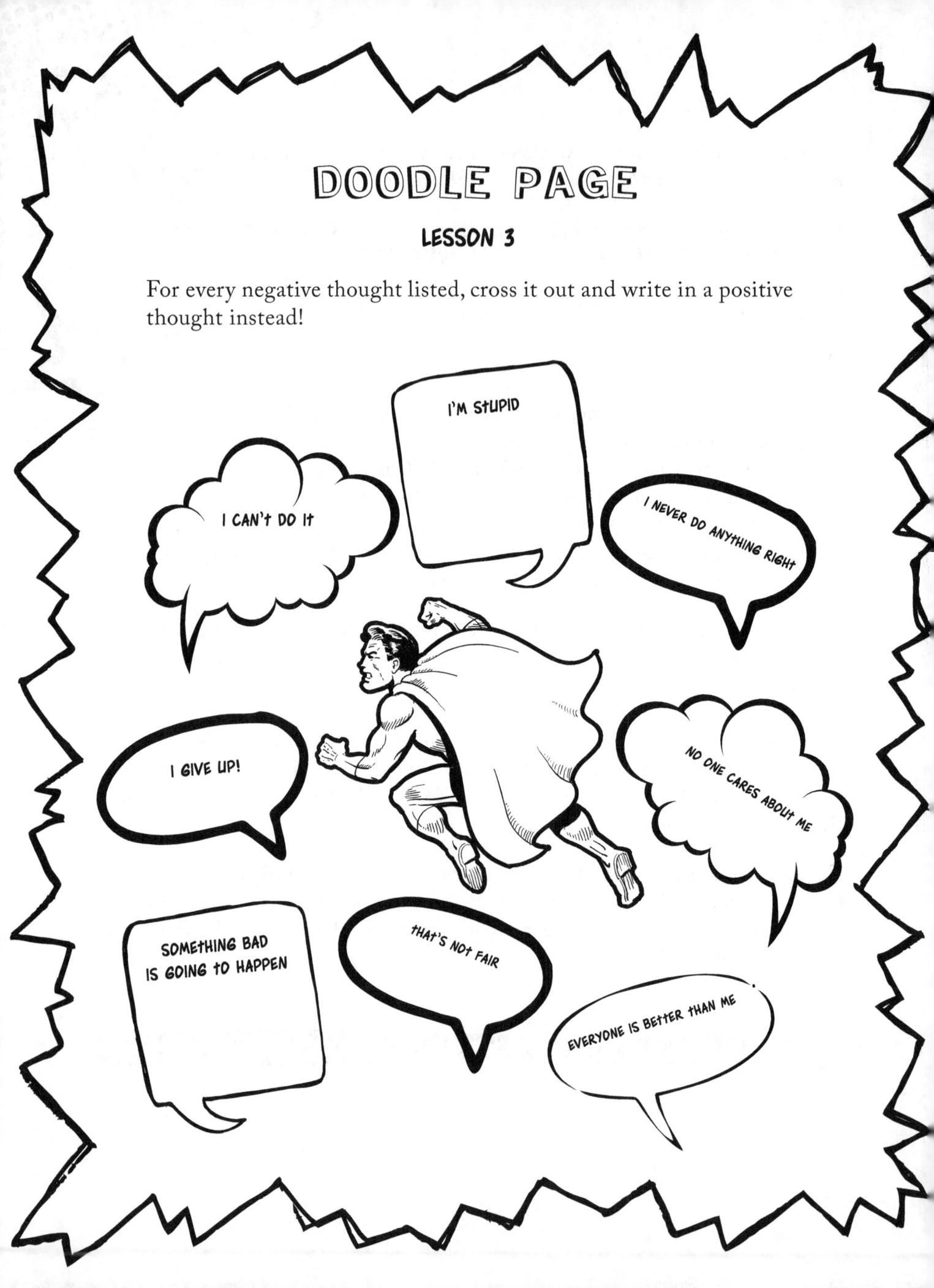

ACTIVITY SHEET

WEEK 3

God wants you to think about good things! In the picture below, circle the GOOD things and put an X through the BAD things.

God wants us to think about good things! In the verse below, fill in the blank with the word that starts with the same letter!

Word List

True

Honorable

Right

Pure

Lovely

Admirable

Excellent

Worthy

"Fix your thoughts on what is T_____, and H_____, and R_____, and P_____, and L_____, and A_____. Think about things that are E_____ and W_____ of praise."

–Philippians 4:8

Now find the words here!

```
Y P W Z W Y C I P D Z X T M A
H U A V A A L Q T R W E N D G
T R M Q Y H Y E S R S B M F S
R E A V J O H O V I U I M T G
O H O W F N A A A O R E W G V
W V X Y W O Y R H A L A F H D
Y F I G F R P T B P A J D P A
Q V Z H O A Z L Z K J N W K Q
D B F M A B E C C U G E S Q D
S X B Y D L T N E L L E C X E
G G W G P E P F L S I V K R G
W Z Y T T J A C G L H Y B L D
Z M W E E H O X R I G H T V B
E M F P R X I N M E V I I A J
P V Q E L C W P B P J J Z G J
```

Word List

Admirable
Excellent
Honorable
Lovely
Praise
Pure
Right
True
Worthy

Look up Proverbs 4:23 in your Bible. Write it out here:

Bazooka Boys ★ Who Am I?

God wants us to be careful with the things we think about. Inside the picture, write some negative things you sometimes think about. Then cross them out and write positive things instead!

WEEK 3

BAZOOKA BREAKDOWN

God doesn't want us thinking about negative things, scary things, bad things or things that make us worried. In the bubble below, write out or draw one thought that you have struggled with which left you sad, scared or nervous.

Bazooka Boys ★ Who Am I?

WEEK 3

When do you struggle most with your thoughts? Circle the answer that most fits or write your own in the space provided.

What is one way you could KICK THE HABIT of thinking bad thoughts during those times? Write your answer here.

KICK THE HABIT!

_____

_____

_____

The "W" plan means we think on things that are true, lovely, pure, excellent, worthy of praise. In the space provided, write one thing that you can think about this week?

I will think about what is::

TRUE _____

LOVELY _____

PURE _____

EXCELLENT _____

WORTHY
OF PRAISE _____

Bazooka Boys ★ Who Am I?

"WHO'S THE BOSS" BALLOON ROCKET

Supplies

- Large balloon
- Tape
- Straw
- Long string (small enough to fit through the straw)
- Chair

Prep

- Tie one end of the string to the back a chair.
- Pre cut tape into 1 inch strips.

Directions

1. Blow up balloons, but don't knot them. Keep the end pinched so no air escapes.
2. Tape the straw to the inflated balloon.
3. Feed the string through the straw.
4. Pull the string tight.
5. Release the end of the balloon end and watch it fly toward the chair.

Romans 8:6 tells us to let the Holy Spirit be "the boss of our brain!"

Bazooka Boys ★ Who Am I?

WATCH YOUR MOUTH

What's the Point?
Our words have power, so we should be careful what we say.

THEME VERSE

Let the words of my mouth and the thoughts of my heart be pleasing to you O Lord.
Psalm 19:14

RELATED BIBLE PASSAGE

James 1:26

Joshua's little sister was SUCH a pain! She was always coming into his room and messing with his stuff. She spied on him and his friends and told everyone their private conversations. She drove him crazy, and the more angry he got, the more she seemed determined to annoy him.

His frustration was growing and growing, and he found himself saying really mean things back at her. He knew it wasn't right, but he couldn't seem to stop himself from screaming at her. He kept trying to justify his reaction by telling himself, "She deserves it!" or "If she would leave me alone, I wouldn't have to yell at her!"

But one day he was reading his Bible when he came across James 1:26: *"You might think you are a very religious person. But if your tongue is out of control, you are fooling yourself"* (ERV).

What does it mean for your **tONGUE** to be out of control? It means you aren't using self-control to make sure the words that come out of your mouth are kind to others and pleasing to God.

Joshua realized the words he was saying to his sister were not okay. Even though he was wrong, it didn't make his behavior any better. He knew that if he wanted to show God how much he loved Him, he would need to do a better job choosing the words he said to his sister.

The Bible tells us over and over again that our words matter. It's crazy how many verses in the Bible are about watching what you say! Why do you think God took the time to talk to us about this?

BECAUSE OUR WORDS ARE POWERFUL.

Think of how you feel when someone says something nice to you. It can change

Bazooka Boys ★ Who Am I?

your whole day! It can make you want to try something new. You feel happy, encouraged, and strong when someone says something good.

Now, think of how you feel when someone says something mean or unkind. IT'S THE WORST! When someone says something hurtful, it can make you feel horrible. Those mean words can stick with you for a really, really long time and make you feel bad about yourself.

Why? Because our words are powerful.

That's why it's so important to be careful about what we say. It can be so easy to have a thought and then let it slip out of your mouth without ever thinking about what those words might do to another person, but the truth is that our words are a big, big deal. Proverbs 13:3 says, *"Those who control their tongue will have a long life; opening your mouth can ruin everything."*

Have you ever squeezed a big glob of toothpaste out of the tube? (Hopefully this was an accident and not something you did on purpose!) Have you ever tried to put toothpaste back into the tube once its been squeezed out? It doesn't work! Once the toothpaste comes out of the tube, you cannot put it back in. It's the same with our words—once they come out, you can't put them back in again. You can apologize and try and make it right, but once the words come out of your mouth, they go right into the hearts of your family members and friends, and you cannot take them back.

Our words have the power to hurt others, and once you say them, you can't take them back. Even if you're really sorry and apologize, the words you said have already done their damage. This is why it's important to learn to control your tongue and **STOP** yourself from saying things you shouldn't say.

So how can we choose good words?

 1. CLEAN WORDS COME FROM A CLEAN HEART.

Luke 6:45 says, "*A good man says good things. These come from the good that is stored up in his heart. An evil man says evil things. These come from the evil that is stored up in his heart. A person's mouth says everything that is in their heart.*" If the words coming out of your mouth are not good words, then you need to look at what's going on in your heart.

If you find yourself saying mean, unkind, or inappropriate words, you need to take a good look at your heart. Are you angry inside? Are you scared about something and lashing out at others? Are you feeling bad about yourself, so it seems okay to hurt others, too? Or maybe you've just gotten careless about choosing the right words and you just let your first thought come out instead of practicing self-control?

If you're having a problem with your words, the first thing to do is to look at your heart. Ask Jesus to take away the bad things in your heart that seem to be coming out of your mouth. Pray the prayer King David prayed in Psalm 51:10: "*Create in me a clean heart, O God.*" A clean heart is the first step to having clean words.

REMEMBER THAT CLEAN WORDS COME FROM A CLEAN HEART.

The second way we can choose good words is to...

 2. STOP TALKING!

So often, we find ourselves saying things we shouldn't. Many times we **KNOW** we shouldn't share that secret or yell at our friend or repeat that word you know is inappropriate, but sometimes we just don't make the right choice in the moment. One of the best ways to help control yourself is simply by saying "**STOP!**"

When you feel yourself starting to say something mean, close your mouth and imagine putting a piece of tape over it. When you start to repeat that juicy piece of gossip about a friend, close your mouth and pretend to lock your lips together and throw away the key. When you're tempted to whine when your mom asks you to set the dinner table, press your lips together **AS TIGHT AS YOU CAN** and repeat inside to yourself, "I will not whine! I will not whine!"

Sometimes the very best thing you can do to control your tongue is just stop talking. There's a verse in the Bible that says, *"A person who talks too much gets into trouble. A wise person learns to be quiet"* (Proverbs 10:19, ERV). A really good way to practice self-control with your words is to simply stop talking when you don't have anything nice to say.

So, clean words come from a clean heart, STOP talking, and lastly...

 3. T.H.I.N.K. BEFORE YOU SPEAK!

So often, we say whatever pops into our heads. We don't stop to think about the words and how they'll affect the people around us. I learned a really great way to check out my words **BEFORE** I say them.

Here's how it works—before you speak, ask yourself, "Is this…"

TRUE?

HELPFUL?

INSPIRING?

NECESSARY?

KIND?

Silas heard the craziest news about his friend Seth—he had failed a math test and his mom was going to have to come into school to talk to the teacher. At recess, a bunch of the boys came over and began asking him questions about Seth. They were sharing all kinds of rumors and gossip about the situation. Some people were saying he cheated, others were saying he was going to be grounded, and others were just laughing.

Silas stopped for a moment and decided to **t.H.I.N.K** before he spoke. First of all, many of the things the guys said were **NOT TRUE**. Secondly, nothing the boys said was **HELPFUL**. It wasn't helping Seth at all to have his friends talking about him when he wasn't there to defend himself. It also wasn't **INSPIRING**. This conversation wasn't focusing on good things, it was focusing on bad things. Silas also wondered if it was **NECESSARY** to talk through the issues with these boys. It didn't seem right to talk about what had happened without Seth being there. And lastly, he asked himself if it was **KIND** to talk to his other friends about something that might be embarrassing to Seth. He realized he would be hurt if the same thing happened to him, so he decided the conversation wasn't **KIND**.

Once Silas went through his **t.H.I.N.K** list, he was convinced he shouldn't be having that conversation. He told the other guys that he didn't think it was cool to talk about this and he turned around and walked away. Although it could have been really easy to just go along with his friends, Silas decided to **t.H.I.N.K**. before he spoke.

Bazooka Boys ★ Who Am I?

Our words are powerful. The things we say can build people up or tear them down. They can make people feel better or make them feel worse. They can honor our parents and teachers, or they can show disrespect. They can be honest, or they can be full of lies. They can be grateful, or they can be whining and complaining.

Colossians 4:6 says, "*Let your conversations always be full of grace and seasoned with salt.*" When something is seasoned with salt, it makes people thirsty! When our conversations are filled with grace (kind and good things), people will be thirsty to know more about Jesus. There's nothing I want more than that! So let's choose our words carefully and practice self-control.

DOODLE PAGE

LESSON 4

Clean words come from a clean heart, in the word bubbles next to the dark heart, write some words that can come from a heart that is not clean. In the word bubbles next to the white heart, write some words that can come from a clean heart.

ACTIVITY SHEET

WEEK 4

Ephesians 4:29 says, *"When you talk, don't say anything bad. But say the good things that people need—whatever will help them grow stronger. Then what you say will be a blessing to those who hear you"* (ERV). Our superheroes are encouraging one another! Write the following words in the bubbles and then color the picture! Good words:

Way to go!

You're amazing!

Nice job!

You're super strong!

61

Look up the following verses in your Bible and write them below:

Psalm 141:3　　　Proverbs 18:21　　　Proverbs 12:14　　　Proverbs 12: 18

Bazooka Boys ★ Who Am I?

Use the key to solve the word problem below.

Ephesians 4:29

A	B	D	E	G	H	I	K	L	M	N	O	P	R	S	T	U	V	W	Y
15	5	23	8	16	19	7	6	14	17	10	11	3	1	26	20	4	21	13	24

"W H E N   Y O U   T A L K ,   D O N ' T
13 19 8 10   24 11 4   20 15 14 6   23 11 10   20

S A Y   A N Y T H I N G   B A D .
26 15 24   15 10 24 20 19 7 10 16   5 15 23

B U T   S A Y   T H E   G O O D
5 4 20   26 15 24   20 19 8   16 11 11 23

T H I N G S   T H A T   P E O P L E
20 19 7 10 16 26   20 19 15 20   3 8 11 3 14 8

N E E D   W H A T E V E R   W I L L
10 8 8 23   13 19 15 20 8 21 8 1   13 7 14 14

H E L P   T H E M   G R O W .
19 8 14 3   20 19 8 17   16 1 11 13

S T R O N G E R   T H E N   W H A T
26 20 1 11 10 16 8 1   20 19 8 10   13 19 15 20

Y O U   S A Y   W I L L   B E   A
24 11 4   26 15 24   13 7 14 14   5 8   15

B L E S S I N G   T O   T H O S E
5 14 8 26 26 7 10 16   20 11   20 19 11 26 8

W H O   H E A R   Y O U ."
13 19 11   19 8 15 1   24 11 4

BAZOOKA BREAKDOWN

What did we learn from the lesson of the tube of toothpaste? Write out your answer on the tube below.

Today we learned that clean words come from a clean heart. What could be going on inside someone's heart to make them say mean words? Write some ideas in the hearts below.

Bazooka Boys ★ Who Am I?

WEEK 4

Do you remember what the T.H.I.N.K principle is? Fill in the blanks below. Look back at the lesson if you need a hint!

T _____

H _____

I _____

N _____

K _____

Copy the theme verse and see if you can memorize it!

"Let the words of my mouth and the thoughts of my heart be pleasing to you O Lord." —Psalm 19:14

THINK LAUNCHER

<u>Supplies</u>

- 3 cardboard tubes (Paper towel sized)
- Wooden Spoon
- 4 rubber bands
- Pom Poms, marshmallows, scrunched up balls of paper or other soft items for launching
- 5 cups labeled with a letter (T. H. I. N. K.)

<u>Directions</u>

1. Lay two of the cardboard tubes side by side and then place the third tube on top to form a triangle shaped stack.

2. Fasten the tubes together with a rubber band on each end.

3. Next, position the wooden spoon at the front of the tubes, and loop a rubber band over the top of the spoon, stretch it around the tubes and then bring it back over itself at the top of the spoon so it holds the spoon to the tubes.

4. Finally, take the last rubber band, loop it over the handle of the wooden spoon, take it around the cardboard tubes, and back over the spoon.

5. Launch the pompoms at the cups. If a pompom lands in a cup, they boy must yell out what that letter means! (True, Helpful, Inspiring, Necessary, Kind)

Bazooka Boys ★ Who Am I?

MONEY MATTERS

What's the Point?
Everything we have comes from God, and we need to do whatever Jesus tells us to do with our money and things

THEME VERSE
And God will generously provide all you need. Then you will always have everything you need and plenty left over to share with others.
2 Corinthians 9:8

RELATED BIBLE PASSAGE
John 6:5–15

Has anyone ever given you money? Maybe you got a five-dollar bill in a birthday card from your grandparents? Or maybe your parents gave you a dollar for doing an extra chore? Or maybe you found a quarter on the ground?

Do you want to hear something really cool? The Bible tells us **GOD** is the one who gives us money. I know that can seem crazy because it seems like our money is given to us by other people. But the truth is, when someone gives you money, they're doing it because God wants them to do it. God is in charge of **ALL** the money in the whole world, and He gives it to us to use for the things He wants us to use it for.

First Chronicles 29:14 says, "*Everything comes from you. We've given back to you only what comes from you.*" And verse 16 of that same chapter says, "*But all of it comes from you. All of it belongs to you*" (NIRV).

God owns all the money in the entire universe, and He gives it to us to use. Another cool verse—Psalm 50:12—says, "*I already own the world and everything in it*" (ERV). Everything in the whole world belongs to God. He's the boss.

One cool thing about God is that He gives us money to buy things. He gives your parents jobs so they can earn money to pay for your house and food. He gives your grandparents money so they can come visit you. He gives **YOU** money to buy toys, treats, and lots of other things.

It's so important to remember that everything we have belongs to God. That means our money and all our things! When we remember that, it changes the way we take care of what we have.

So what does it mean to have self-control with

oOOooOooOoo oOOo oOoo OooOoOOo

our money and the other things God has given us to take care of? Practicing self-control means we don't do things without thinking—and we make sure we do the things God wants us to do! When it comes to our

Bazooka Boys ★ Who Am I?

money, we need to make sure we think about the way God wants us to use the things he's given us to hold.

What are some ways we can have self-control with our money and things?

1. GIVE BACK TO GOD WHAT HE ASKS YOU TO GIVE.

Andrew saw his mom with a calculator, her computer, and a checkbook. He asked his mom what she was doing, and she said, "I'm paying bills." Andrew was curious, so he asked, "What's the very first bill you pay?" Andrew's mom replied, "Oh, that's easy. The very first check I write is to our church! I know God has provided money for our family, so I make sure I give my very first offering to Him!"

Have you ever heard the word "tithe"? It's a funny word that comes up several times in the Bible. The first place it's mentioned is in Deuteronomy 14:22–23, which says, *"You must set aside a tithe of your crops—one-tenth of all the crops you harvest each year. Bring this tithe to the designated place of worship…"* People would bring the **VERY** best of their crops and animals to the Temple and give them back to God. They brought ten percent of everything they grew as an offering to God! When we tithe, we're reminding ourselves that all our money **REALLY** belongs to God. It's a way of saying **"THANK YOU"** for all the things He's provided for us!

Now what that means is that whatever money you and I get, we give ten percent back to God's work. Most people give their tithes to the church they go to. Churches use that money to help tell other people about Jesus. So when you tithe, you're helping the people in your community hear how much Jesus loves them.

THAT'S A PRETTY AWESOME WAY TO SPEND YOUR MONEY!

The second way you can practice self-control with your money is to…

 ## 2. TAKE CARE OF THE STUFF GOD GIVES YOU!

God has given you and me so many things, and one way we can show Him our appreciation is by taking good care of the stuff He gives us. That means not destroying things. That means not being wasteful with food, or toys, or lots of other stuff. It also means being responsible for the things God has put us in charge of. When we show respect for the things God has given us, it's another way of saying "Thank You!" to God for being so generous with us!

And the last way we can practice self-control with our money is to…

 ## 3. BE GENEROUS.

God gives us money so we can pay our bills, have food to eat, and have clothes to wear. But He also gives us money so we can use it to help other people. We need to always ask Jesus if there's anything special He wants us to do with His money.

There's a story in the Bible about a little boy who was determined to share what he had with Jesus to help other people. Jesus was teaching lots of people—around 4,000 of them! They had been sitting there for a long time, and they were all starting to get really, really hungry! There were no restaurants in those days (So sad—no McDonalds!). Everyone was wondering what to do when a little boy came to Jesus and said, "I will share my lunch!" So Jesus took the boy's lunch, which had five loaves of bread and two fish in it, and prayed over it. Then the coolest miracle happened—God multiplied the food, and there was enough to feed every single person with baskets of food left over!

What I love about this story is that the little boy was willing to share what He had to help others. God has given you lots and lots of things, and He wants you to use those things to help others. So be generous, and always ask

Jesus if He wants you to share something you have with someone else. Matthew 10:42 says, *"And if you give even a cup of cold water to one of the least of my followers, you will surely be rewarded."* God might ask you to give someone food, it might be money, it might even be something as simple as a cup of water. But whatever Jesus asks you to do, just do it!

One really important thing to remember when we talk about having self-control with our money is that we need to be really careful how we use the things God has given us.

It's so fun to have money to spend! As soon as that money finds its way into your pocket, you start imagining all the things you can buy with your cash. Maybe you love to buy gum or candy. Maybe you want to save up for a special toy. Or maybe you want to spend your money on a gift for someone you care about.

But **BEFORE** you do that, God wants you to **STOP, THINK**, and **ASK** Him how He wants you to handle your money. Too often we just go and spend all our money without thinking. Many of us run out and spend our money and then think about it later. But a really good rule to remember is to **THINK** first, and spend second. Think, "Is this what God wants me to do with my money? Does He want me to be generous to someone first? Should I save this money to buy something bigger later? Are my parents okay with me spending my money this way?"

DON'T JUST SPEND WITHOUT THINKING! THINK FIRST, AND THEN SPEND!

God wants us to do three things with our money: Share. Save. Spend. Share what you have with God and others. Then save some money for things you may need later. And then spend and enjoy what God has provided for you!

DOODLE PAGE

LESSON 5

A good way to take care of the money God gives us is to share, spend, and save! On the list below draw a picture of something you could share! Draw a picture of something you could save up for! And then draw a picture of something you want to spend your money on after you've been generous!

SHARE

SPEND

SAVE

ACTIVITY SHEET

WEEK 5

John 6:1–15 tells the story of the little boy who shared his lunch with Jesus. Jesus took the fish and bread the boy gave Him and multiplied it to feed thousands of people! On the fish below, draw a picture or write out some things you have that you could share with others.

Our theme verse this week is 2 Corinthians 9:8. In the sentence below, write the word **NEED** in the blank spaces, then practice reading the verse out loud.

"And God will generously provide all you _____. Then you will always have everything you _____ and plenty left over to share with others" (2 Corinthians 9:8).

Use the words about money and generosity below to complete the crossword puzzle.

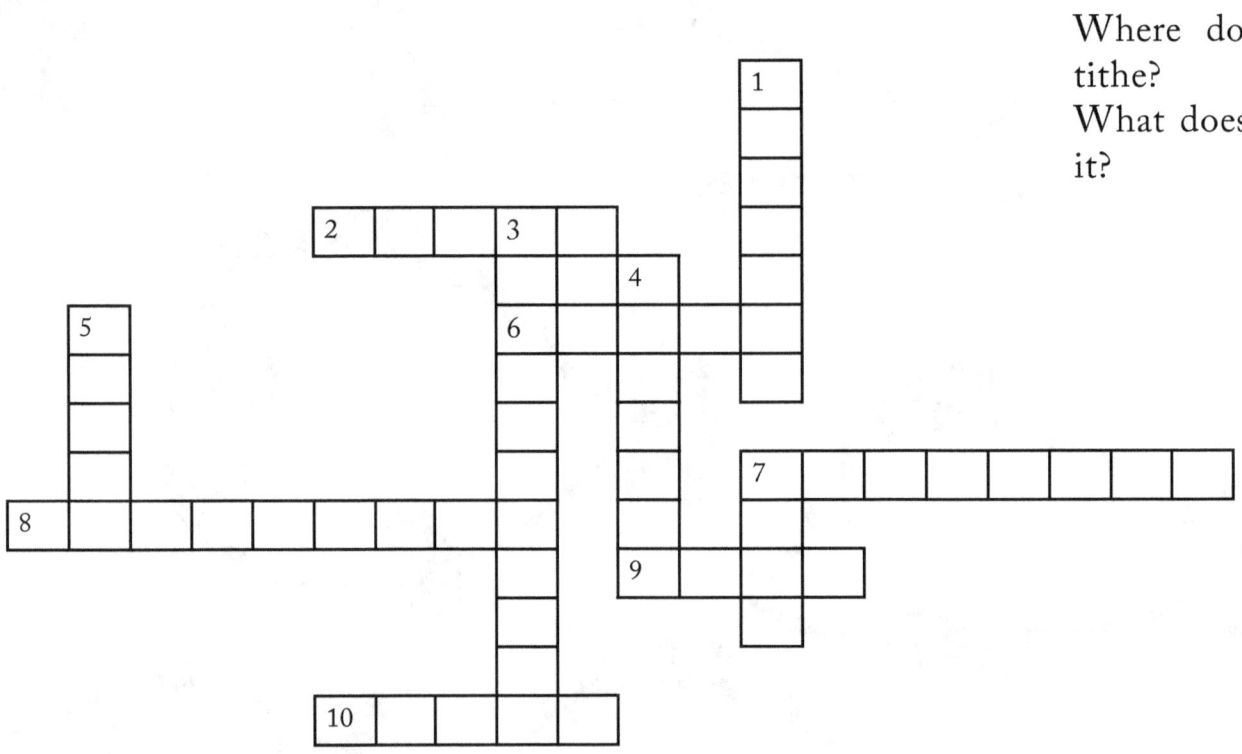

Where do we give tithe?
What does God do it?

Across
2. share
6. spend
7. generous
8. resources
9. save
10. money

Down
1. provide
3. responsible
4. belongs
5. tithe
7. give

Bazooka Boys ★ Who Am I?

BAZOOKA BREAKDOWN

WEEK 5

One of the biggest ways we can practice self-control with our money is by giving back to God what belongs to him! Answer the following questions:

1.

2.

3.

Another way we can practice self-control with our money is by taking care of the stuff God gives us. What are some ways we can take care of the things God has given us?

What three things did we learn today to help us take care of the money God gives us? Fill in the blanks below!

S_____

S_____

S_____

WEEK 5

DUCT TAPE WALLETS

<u>Supplies</u>

- Plain or patterned Duct tape (approx. 10 ft.)
- Scissors
- Ruler

<u>Directions</u>

1. Cut four 10 inch strips of duct tape and create a wide sheet by overlapping the edges.
2. Repeat step one and then place the two sticky sides of the sheets together to create the main part of your wallet.
3. Next, cut two 3 inch pieces of duct tape and place them sticky sides together to create your pocket. If desired, cut a contrasting piece of tape and fold over the top to make a fun edge.
4. Repeat step three so you have two pocket pieces.
5. Fold over your large sheet to create a long, skinny rectangle.
6. Place the 3 inch piece on the front left side of the wallet. Place the second 3 inch piece on the front right side of the wallet. Cut a 11 or 12 inch strip and place along the bottom of the wallet, half of the strip on the front and half on the back. Fold up the strip to secure the pockets in place. Trim the edges if necessary.
7. Cut a 7 inch piece of duct tape and place on the side of the wallet – half on the front and half on the back. Secure and trim as necessary. Repeat on the other side.

1.

2. Sticky sides together.

3. Sticky sides together.

Optional: *fold*

4. Sticky sides together.

5. *fold*

6. *fold* — trim

7. *fold*   *fold*

USING MY GIFTS

What's the Point?
God has given each of us things we're good at, and we need to make sure we're doing everything we can to use our gifts!

THEME VERSE
*God has given each of you a gift from his great variety of **spiritual** gifts.*
1 Peter 4:10

RELATED BIBLE PASSAGE
Matthew 25:14–30

Is there something you're REALLY good at doing? Maybe it's playing an instrument or doing science experiments? Maybe you love to read books or bake cakes? Maybe you love to fix things or play soccer?

Every single one of us has things we're good at—EVERY SINGLE ONE OF US. You know how I know that? Because the Bible tells us God has given each of us a gift or a talent. First Peter 4:10 says, *"God has given each of you a gift from his great variety of spiritual gifts. Use them well to serve one another."* That means when God created you, He made you good at certain things. Your gifts are probably different from my gifts, but you can be sure that God has put gifts inside of YOU!

Wasn't that so nice of God? I think it's pretty cool that He chose to give us things that would bring us so much joy! Our world could have just been filled with boring things that we all felt kind of excited about. Instead, He gave us things that we love, love, love to do!

And because we know our gifts were GIVEN to us by God, we can know God wants us to use our gifts the VERY best way we can. He wants us to work hard and practice and use them as much as possible. So when we talk about having self-control in every area of our lives, we should ask ourselves: Am I being self-controlled in the way I use my gifts?

God gave us talents, and He wants us to USE them. Imagine you pick out a gift for your mom for her birthday. You spend hours thinking about what you're going to get her. Then you spend hours shopping for just the right color and shape. And then you even go above the amount you were planning to spend just because you want to make her day extra special. You give it to her and you're so excited to give her such a special present.

Bazooka Boys ★ Who Am I?

A month later, you see the gift just sitting in the corner, still in the box, gathering dust. I can imagine you'd be pretty frustrated. You might think, "Hey, I spent a lot of time and energy on that gift, and you're doing **NOTHING** with it." I don't think you'd be very happy.

Some of you aren't taking very good care of the gifts God has given you. They're sitting on a shelf, gathering dust. You're not using the gifts and talents God has placed inside of you. I bet it makes God pretty sad to see gifts He's given us just sitting on the shelf, not being used or taken care of.

There's actually a story in the Bible where Jesus shares how He feels when people neglect the gifts and responsibilities He has given them.

Parable of the Talents Matthew 25:14–30, NIRV)

> *"At that time God's kingdom will also be like a man leaving home to travel to another place for a visit. Before he left, he talked with his servants. He told his servants to take care of his things while he was gone. He decided how much each servant would be able to care for. The man gave one servant five bags of money. He gave another servant two bags. And he gave a third servant one bag. Then he left. The servant who got five bags went quickly to invest the money. Those five bags of money earned five more. It was the same with the servant who had two bags. That servant invested the money and earned two more. But the servant who got one bag of money went away and dug a hole in the ground. Then he hid his master's money in the hole.*
>
> *After a long time the master came home. He asked the servants what they did with his money. The servant who got five bags brought that amount and five more bags of money to the master. The servant said, 'Master, you trusted me to care for five bags of money. So I used them*

to earn five more.' The master answered, 'You did right. You are a good servant who can be trusted. You did well with that small amount of money. So I will let you care for much greater things. Come and share my happiness with me.' Then the servant who got two bags of money came to the master. The servant said, 'Master, you gave me two bags of money to care for. So I used your two bags to earn two more.' The master answered, 'You did right. You are a good servant who can be trusted. You did well with a small amount of money. So I will let you care for much greater things. Come and share my happiness with me.' Then the servant who got one bag of money came to the master. The servant said, 'Master, I knew you were a very hard man. You harvest what you did not plant. You gather crops where you did not put any seed. So I was afraid. I went and hid your money in the ground. Here is the one bag of money you gave me.' The master answered, 'You are a bad and lazy servant! You say you knew that I harvest what I did not plant and that I gather crops where I did not put any seed. So you should have put my money in the bank. Then, when I came home, I would get my money back. And I would also get the interest that my money earned.' So the master told his other servants, 'Take the one bag of money from that servant and give it to the servant who has ten bags. Everyone who uses what they have will get more. They will have much more than they need. But people who do not use what they have will have everything taken away from them" (Matthew 25:14–30, NIRV).

YIKES!

This story is a great example of how God feels when we don't use the gifts He's given us. The master in the story called the servant who didn't use his talents a "bad and lazy servant." I don't know about you, but I don't want to be a "bad and lazy servant"! I want to be a good servant who works hard at my gifts. God gave us gifts to use…so we should use them to the best of our abilities.

Bazooka Boys ★ Who Am I?

How can we have self-control when it comes to our gifts? How can we make sure we're doing the hard work and being a faithful servant with our talents?

1. DISCOVER YOUR GIFTS.

We've already learned EVERYONE has gifts from God. And we've learned that everyone's gifts are different from everyone else's. The first thing we should do to be faithful with our gifts is to discover what they are!

What are your gifts?

What are you good at?

What makes you happy?

What are some things that come really easy to you?

What kind of things do you like learning about?

What do you do for fun?

At the end of this lesson, we have a quiz that will help you figure it out. Take the quiz, make a list, or ask your friends and family what talents or gifts they see in you. They may have some great ideas!

Lucas didn't think he had any gifts. He didn't like to sing or play piano. He didn't like to draw or play soccer like his friends. He always thought gifts were just things you did in music or art class. But one day his mom commented on how God had given him the gift of compassion. He wasn't sure what that meant, so he asked his mom to explain. His mom said, "Someone with the gift of compassion notices when other people are sad and hurt and wants to help. You always think about other people and go out of your way to make sure they're okay. Not everyone thinks that way, Lucas. God made you especially sensitive to other people's feelings so you could reach out and help them. It's a special gift, and it is awesome!"

This was a such a cool moment for Lucas! As far back as he could remember, he had a heart for those who were hurting. It was never something he had to try to do—it was part of who he is.

For some reason, it had never occurred to him that this wasn't an accident. Part of God's design and plan for his life was a soft heart toward people!

This totally changed Lucas's life. From that moment on, he paid close attention when his heart was sad for another person. Instead of ignoring the feeling or simply brushing it off, he looked at it as a mission from heaven to reach out to the person God had put in his path.

Maybe your gift is that you care for people like Lucas. Maybe you're good at teaching other people. Maybe you're good at playing a certain sport or instrument. Maybe your gift is leading other people, or maybe you love to organize things.

The first way you can make sure you are using self-control with your gifts is to make sure you know what they are. Once you know what you're passionate about, the second thing you need to do is…

 ## 2. PRACTICE, PRACTICE, PRACTICE!

Jackson LOVES to play the violin. He started taking lessons when he was little, and he could tell right away that he's good at it. He didn't even have to try very hard when he first started. The music just flew right out of his fingers!

Then his teacher started giving him harder music to play, and he had to spend extra time practicing every day. Pretty soon, he started whining and complaining whenever it was time to practice. His mom got frustrated, and eventually Jackson would get to it, but he didn't have a very good attitude.

Jackson's story probably sounds familiar. A lot of us have talents that we're excited to use at first, but having natural talent is only the very beginning of having gifts. We have to practice, learn, and study if we want to grow. That takes a lot of hard work and self-control.

Some of you are really gifted at something, but you've stopped working hard at growing in your gifts. You're not practicing hard. You're not studying. You're not working hard to get better. The truth is, when it comes to your talent, you'll only get out of it what you put into it. If you're not working at growing your gift, you'll stay at the level you've always been.

But if you practice hard, you'll get better. If you keep working every day, you'll grow stronger. You'll be like the servant in the story who pleased the Master because he worked hard to make sure he used what he'd been given and multiplied it into something more.

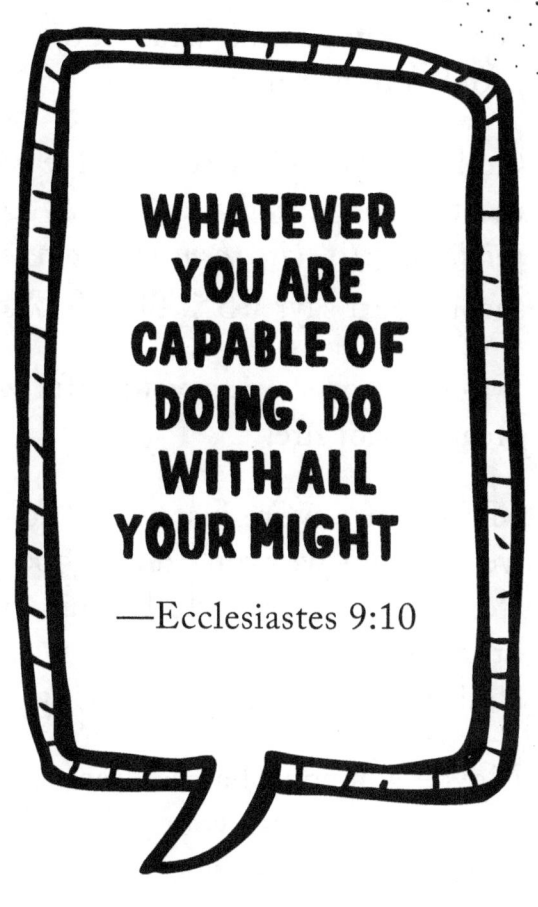

> WHATEVER YOU ARE CAPABLE OF DOING, DO WITH ALL YOUR MIGHT
>
> —Ecclesiastes 9:10

Ecclesiastes 9:10 says, *"Whatever you are capable of doing, do with all your might..."* That means you work your hardest. You practice every day. You go to classes and lessons and ask questions so you can get better.

So, we need to discover our gifts, practice hard, and lastly...

 ## 3. SHARE OUR GIFTS WITH OTHERS!

I think there are a lot of people in the world who **KNOW** what their gifts are, but they're too scared to **SHARE** their gifts with others. Maybe they love to sing but would **NEVER** sing in front of other people. Maybe they **LOVE** to play basketball in the yard with their family, but they're too nervous to join a team and play when other people are watching. Maybe they love to build things, but they never show anyone what they've made because they're scared of what other people might think.

God gave you gifts because He wants you to use them to help others! Look at our theme verse again: "*God has given each of you a gift from his great variety of spiritual gifts. Use them well to serve one another*" (1 Peter 4:10). What does that second part say? USE THEM WELL TO SERVE ONE ANOTHER!

If you're not sharing your gifts with others, you're missing out on one of the great joys of life!

Many times we're just scared to use our gifts. We don't want to look silly, or we're afraid we won't do a good job. Remember the third servant in the our story in Matthew? He hid his gift! He said, "I was afraid." He was afraid of other people's reactions. He was afraid of failing. He was unsure of his own abilities. He just stopped trying.

Maybe someone has said something mean to you or made fun of you when you've tried to use your gift in the past. Sometimes it can be hard to get past a bad experience. Maybe someone has mistreated your gift.

I know this can be so hard, but don't fall for it! Don't allow someone else to keep you from what God has for you. Even if it's scary, remind yourself that God has plans for you and your talents.

When I've faced this situation, it's helped me to refocus my attention away from what **OTHER** people think of me and determine that it is far more important for me to please my Heavenly Father than any other person. I remember Galatians 1:10: "*If I were still trying to please men, I would not be Christ's servant.*" Do not allow another person to convince you that your gift has no value. Do not let your fear of what other people might say keep you sidelined. Decide to use your talents as a faithful servant of Jesus, and let Him deal with the people who would try to discourage you.

If your gift is sitting on a shelf gathering dust, it's time to take it down and start using it again!

First Timothy 4:14–16 says, "*...that special gift of ministry you were given when the leaders of the church laid hands on you and prayed—keep that dusted off and in use. Cultivate these things. Immerse yourself in them. The people will all see you mature right before their eyes! Keep a firm grasp on both your character and your teaching. Don't be diverted. Just keep at it*" (MSG).

God has given you gifts. Discover what they are. Faithfully practice and grow them. Faithfully share them with others.

DOODLE PAGE

LESSON 6

Everyone has gifts! In the boxes below, write out (or draw a picture of) 3 things that you are good at. Then in the boxes underneath, write out one way you can work hard to use that gift!

ACTIVITY SHEET

WEEK 6

Look up 1 Peter 4:10 in your Bible and write it in the space provided.

Fill in the blanks to help discover your gifts and talents.

If I have an afternoon to myself, I love to _____.

My favorite subject in school is _____.

If I could volunteer to help somewhere, I would choose to help with _____.

I love to _____.

I want to learn more about _____.

My favorite hobbies are _____.

I'm happiest when I'm _____.

People say that I'm _____.

I feel really proud when I'm _____.

Here's a list of some gifts and talents. Circle anything you're good at.

Being kind

Caring about other people

Movies
(reviewing, writing, filming, story, acting)

Photography

Author (writing stories or articles)

Technology
(setting up blogs, fixing computers)

Thinking
(arguing, debating, worldview, philosophy)

Politics and government

Being responsible

Friendship

Helping your family or teachers

Taking care of God's creation

Telling others about Jesus

Starting new things

Memorizing things

Music

Sports

School

Science

Reading

Inventing

Listening to other people's problems

Visiting people who are sick or sad

Doing thoughtful things for others

Building things

Smiling

Going on adventures

Acting or drama

Art (drawing, painting, making)

Board games, strategy games

Building, construction, carpentry

Organizing things

Solving puzzles and mysteries

Leading a group

Giving things to others

Sharing

Praying for others

Studying the Bible

Teaching

Cooking

Crafts

Electronics
(computers, coding, video games)

Fashion design, sewing

Gardening (veggies, herbs, flowers)

Graphics Arts
(typography, Illustrator, Photoshop)

House renovations and maintenance

Interior decorating

Mechanics
(small motors, fixing things)

Bazooka Boys ★ Who Am I?

Of the things you circled, write your three FAVORITES below:

1.

2.

3.

In the space provided, write out three things you can do to get better at your gifts.

1.

2.

3.

What are three ways you could start using your gifts RIGHT NOW?

Where do our gifts come from? Does everyone have one?

Copy the theme verse in the space provided. See if you can memorize it!

"God has given each of you a gift from his great variety of spiritual gifts. Use them well to serve one another."
1 Peter 4:10

Bazooka Boys ★ Who Am I?

WEEK 6

Think of one thing you're good at. Maybe it's a talent, a sport, a hobby, something at school, or even something about your personality that's unique and brings you or others joy. Draw a picture of yourself doing it in the space provided!

What are some ways we can grow in our gifts? Write 3 ideas in the boxes below.

GOD'S GIFT BINGO

(20 minutes)

Supplies
- Copy paper
- Cardstock
- Gluesticks
- Scissors
- Candy to use as markers
- Container to hold drawing pieces

Prep
- Photocopy gift squares sheets onto copy paper (multiple copies of each sheet)
- Photocopy blank bingo cards onto cardstock (one for each boy)
- Precut the gift squares.
- Place one set of all the gift squares into a container for calling bingo.

Directions

1. Have each boy select 8 "gift squares" that represent something they are good at or interested in.

2. Glue their gift squares onto their bingo card.

3. Give each boy candy to use as markers.

4. Have each player put a marker on their free space.

5. Have the leader draw from the gift squares container and call out the gift. Boys can mark their bingo card when their "gift" is called.

6. Any player that get 3 in a row (horizontal, vertical, or diagonal) calls Bingo and gets to eat their candy!

7. Continue game until all players have achieved bingo!

Bazooka Boys ★ Who Am I?

GOD'S GIFT BINGO

TAKING MY TIME

WHAT'S THE POINT?
God wants us to be smart about how we use our time.

THEME VERSE

There is a right time for everything...
Ecclesiastes 3:1 (ERV)

RELATED BIBLE PASSAGE

Daniel 1:17–21

Do you know how many hours are in a day? **24**.

Do you know how many minutes are in a day? **1,440**.

Do you know how many seconds are in a day? **86,400**.

When God made the world, He started **TIME**. He caused the sun to rise in the morning and set in the evening, created morning and night, and gave us days and weeks and years. **TIME** is something God created.

He gives each and every one of us the same amount of hours, minutes, and seconds in a day. No one gets more. No one gets less. You can't buy more hours for your day.

God wants us to be smart about how we use the time He has given us. Psalm 90:12 says, *"Teach us to number our days, that we may gain a heart of wisdom."* God wants us to realize that every day is precious and we need to make good use of the time He has given us.

God has a plan for every single day of your life. Not one day is wasted. There's not one day that's unimportant. Psalm 139:16 says, *"Every day of my life was recorded in Your book. Every moment was laid out before a single day had passed."* Every day is important and filled with things God has planned for you to do!

So **WHY** is it so easy to manage our time poorly?

WHY do we sometimes waste too much time on things that aren't important?

WHY do we sometimes waste time doing the things we know we shouldn't be doing?

Andrew was having a hard time managing his time. Most of his days looked like this: His Mom would wake him up for school, but he would have a hard time getting up. (He had stayed up extra late the night before playing video games, so he was just

SO tired!) He would lie in bed until he was late and his Mom would yell at him from the kitchen. He would race out of bed, grab some dirty, wrinkly clothes, and race down to breakfast. After he ate, he would run to put his lunch in his backpack and realize he had forgotten to do yesterday's homework assignment! He had meant to do it, but when he got home, he got distracted by his iPad and never got back to it. Oops.

As Andrew raced onto the bus, he wasn't feeling very good about himself. Why was he always forgetting things? Why was he always late? Why couldn't he get his act together?

The truth is, that Andrew was not practicing self-control when it came to his time. He wasn't making good choices about how he spent his minutes. He just went with whatever he felt like doing in the moment instead of making decisions based on what was the best use of his time. He needed to make a plan to manage his time better and then stick to it!

God wants us to be wise with the time He has given us every day. Here are three places we need to have self-control with our time.

 # 1. HAVE SELF-CONTROL IN YOUR WORK TIME.

Do you have a job? I'm guessing that none of you get up in the morning, put on a suit and grab a briefcase, and head out to work! But you **DO** have work that you are responsible for every single day—going to school and doing your very best with your studies, chores and responsibilities at home, things you're committed to (sports teams, music lessons, other clubs or classes).

The first and most important area where you learn to manage your time well is your work. God wants you to be a hard worker. Colossians 3:23 says, *"In all the work you are given, do the best you can. Work as though you are working for the Lord, not any earthly master."* (ERV).

God wants you to work hard! He wants you to do your very best. He wants you to be dependable and responsible. There are lots of reasons this is important, but do you know one of the most important reasons you should be self-controlled with your time? It's is a great way to show others you love Jesus!

There's a story in the Bible about a boy named Daniel and his friends, who were captured and taken to Babylon to be put in the king's service. Everyone watched to see how these four young men would handle this tough situation. This is what the Bible says about Daniel and his friends:

"*Every time the king asked them about something important, they showed great wisdom and understanding. The king found they were ten times better than all the magicians and wise men in his kingdom*" (Daniel 1:20, ERV).

The King and all the other people in the kingdom took note that Daniel and his friends were smart, helpful, and worked hard. It didn't matter what kind of situation they were in, they determined to do their very best no matter what.

My prayer is that any teacher, coach, or friend you have contact with finds you ten times better than anyone else around—just like Daniel! When they ask you why, you'll be able to share that you work hard because you love God and the Bible tells you to!

A lot of people WANT to be ten times better at stuff, but they're not willing to do the hard work to get there. Proverbs 13:4 says, "*Lazy people always want things but never get them. Those who work hard get plenty*" (ERV). So make sure you're studying hard. Make sure you're practicing what you're supposed to be practicing. Make sure you show up on time and don't skip out on things you've committed to.

Bazooka Boys ★ Who Am I?

Determine to be a hard worker today! Show up on time. Get your homework done. Make sure you do your chores well, and without complaining. Be a good manager of your time.

2. HAVE SELF-CONTROL IN YOUR PLAY TIME.

Ben was so excited for Saturday, he could hardly wait! He had a long week at school with so much homework that he couldn't wait to have a day off. He started a marathon of one of his favorite games on his computer, and he just kept playing and playing and playing. After a while, he started feeling kind of yucky. His muscles were feeling sore and he was feeling super blah. His mom came upstairs and asked him how long he had been playing his game, and Ben realized it had been four hours! His mom was not very happy with him, and he was not very happy with himself, either.

How many of you have limits on your computer or iPad time? How many of you have rules about how much TV you can watch? How many of you have rules about how many video games you can play? Why do you think your parents give you rules like that?

It's not good for us to spend too much time doing those things. It's super fun to be able to play fun games and watch good movies or TV shows, but many of us have a hard time practicing self-control. Sometimes we do it as **LONG** as we can get away with (before our parents realize what we've been doing), but I want to challenge you—**YOU** are supposed to be the one who shows self-control with your time. **YOU** are in charge of the minutes God has given you. Instead of just trying to get away with as much as you can get away with, think about what a healthy time limit is and talk about it with

> "LAZY PEOPLE ALWAYS WANT THINGS BUT NEVER GET THEM. THOSE WHO WORK HARD GET PLENTY"
> –Proverbs 13:4 (ERV)

your parents. Then **YOU** take responsibility for staying within those time limits. Maybe you need to set a timer for yourself. Maybe you need to commit to watching one episode of something at a time instead of watching 25!

One of the BIGGEST ways you can practice self-control is by making good choices in how you handle your play time!

And the last way you can practice self-control with your time is to…

 ## 3. HAVE SELF-CONTROL IN YOUR REST TIME.

Have you ever thought about how weird it is that we all **SLEEP** every night? It gets dark outside, we all go into our rooms and crawl into bed, and we pretty much don't know what's going on around us for eight or nine hours. It's weird!

But God designed our bodies to need sleep and God designed our bodies to need rest! If our bodies and minds don't have time to just check out and recover, pretty soon they start wearing down and getting sick. So we need to practice self-control in how we rest!

That means you need to make sure you're getting enough sleep! Remember our story about Andrew, who had such a hard time getting out of bed? Part of his problem was that he wasn't making good choices about getting enough sleep so he could work hard the next day. He was simply doing what he wanted to do at the moment without thinking about how it would affect his ability to do his best at school the next day. (Hmm…Do you remember learning about "I want what I want when I want it"? Seems like Andrew needs to push down the flesh and have self-control!) God wants you to do your best every day. That starts with doing your best to get a good night's sleep.

Another really important way God wants us to rest is by observing a **SABBATH**. Do you know what a Sabbath is? It's kind of a funny word! A Sabbath is a day set aside to rest. The word Sabbath actually means "to stop"! We first read about it in Exodus 20:8–10: *"You must remember to keep the Sabbath a special day. You may work six days a week to do your job. But the seventh day is a day of rest in honor of the Lord your God"* (ERV).

This is actually one of the Ten Commandments! (Which, surprisingly, most of us don't do a very good job at keeping! I'm glad we don't take this same approach with "thou shall not kill!")

Basically, a Sabbath is a day when we take the time to rest and worship. We step away from our normal routine and allow ourselves time to reflect, connect with our families, and rest our bodies.

The Bible is very clear that you and I should set aside time every single week for **REST**. Now, resting might mean taking a nice long nap for some of us, but resting can mean a whole lot of other things, too. You can rest by going for a nice walk with your family. You can rest by cooking a meal or playing a game. You can rest by reading a book or throwing around a baseball. Resting means doing something you enjoy in a relaxed environment. Think about what makes you feel refreshed and ready to take on another day. Whatever those things are, you should make sure you take the time to do those things once a week.

At our house, we have a Sabbath on most Sundays. When we wake up, we have a family rule that no one uses electronics for the morning. This is just something we do to remind us that it's a day to rest and do things differently. Then we go to church and spend time learning about God. Then we try and have a family meal together to talk about the next week and all that's coming up. Then we each do some things that we personally enjoy.

Everybody's Sabbath may look different. Your family may have a Saturday night Sabbath where you have family time and rest. Maybe you have some quiet time during another part of the week. Talk to your parents about ways you can plan some rest time into your family routine every week. God wants to take good care of us, and He tells us over and over in the Bible that we should make sure we have self-control when it comes to having times of rest!

God wants you to have discipline when it comes to your time. Whether you're at work, at play, or at rest, do your very best with the time God has given you every single day!

DOODLE PAGE

LESSON 7

Write a list or draw a picture of 3 things you need to do today.

Write a list or draw a picture of 3 things you want to do today.

Number your items in the order in which you should do them.

ACTIVITY SHEET

On the clock below, draw a picture or write a list of some things you do for your work time, play time, and rest time every day.

Bazooka Boys ★ Who Am I?

Use the word list below to fill in the blanks and complete these verses.

Psalm 139:16

Every _____ of my life was recorded in Your book.

Every _____ was laid out before a single had passed.

Ecclesiastes 3:1

There is a right _____ for everything.

Psalm 90:12

Teach us to number our days that we may gain a heart of _____.

Colossians 3:23

In all the _____ you are given, do the best you can. Work as though you are working for the Lord, not any earthly master.

Proverbs 13:4

_____ people always want things but never get them. Those who work hard get plenty.

Exodus 20:8

You must remember to keep the _____ as a special day.

Word List:

Sabbath	*Lazy*	*Day*
Time	*Wisdom*	
Day	*Work*	

Find the words in the puzzle below!

```
V S M Z P Y E C T T H C Y V S
M R P T I M Z K X H H K A P Z
R T D Q X T P A E U T A D D Z
H O U R S N O R L X A H Y U F
T O F H J I G J C R B T K K N
Z P L U H S M Z E W B P B U Q
S R I G S M W C X T A Y A L P
P O V J Z Y B V N V S L V H N
R R I U W J U Z N P P I V H M
C D E Y A O B Y F Y Q M Y O V
W L G W P H T O H J S G D R F
I A O P Z T I Y L S T S N J M
J R K C U A M F N R I D D G I
K X X Z K F E J L W V L L B T
V C Z R A P I E A I D C V P N
```

Word List:

Clock

Day

Hours

Lazy

Play

Sabbath

Time

Wisdom

Work

Bazooka Boys ★ Who Am I?

Read the story of Daniel in Daniel 1. In the blanks below, write three things Daniel did that set him apart from all the other people.

1. _____

2. _____

3. _____

What can you learn from Daniel's example?

BAZOOKA BREAKDOWN

What is your **WORK**? In other words, what are the responsibilities you have every day? (School, chores, practice, lessons, etc) Write them in the left column. What are some ways you can have more self-control in your work? Write your answers in the right column!

WORK	WAYS TO HAVE MORE SELF-CONTROL

WEEK 7

When it comes to your playtime, what is the thing that is hardest for you to practice self-control? Write it in the TV screen. What can you do to be better about limits during your playtime? Write your ideas on the blank lines.

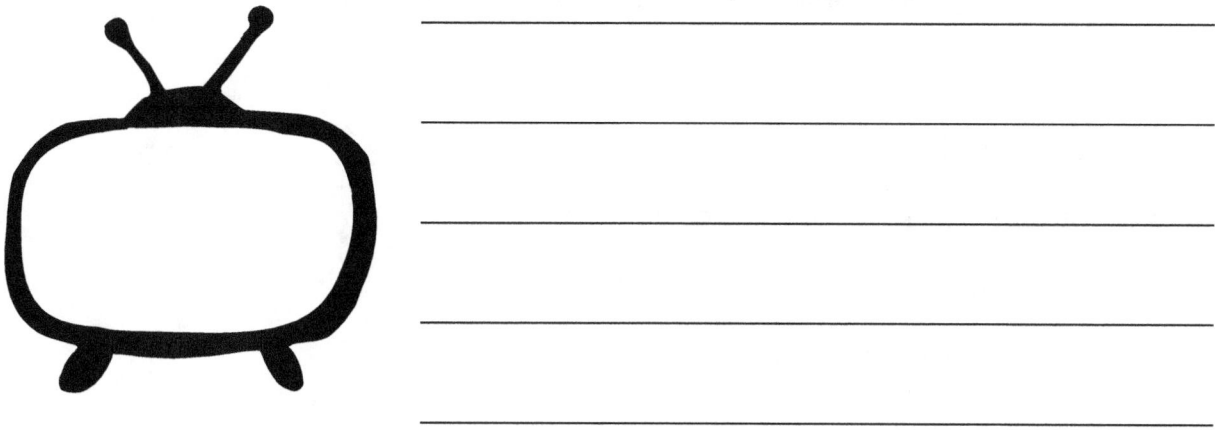

A Sabbath is taking time every day to rest. Draw a picture of what you would do during your rest time.

TAKING MY TIME DOORHANGER

<u>Supplies</u>

- Foam Door Hanger
- Permanent Markers (variety of colors)
- Wooden Clothes Pins (5 or 6 per boy)
- Foam Stickers (optional)

<u>Directions</u>

1. Use a permanent marker to write on the foam door hanger:
   – Write "**TO DO**" on the left side under the opening.
   – Write "**DONE**" on the right side under the opening.

2. Use a permanent marker to write different types of chores on each clothes pin (brush teeth, make bed, take out garbage, load dishes, unload dishes, read, etc.).

3. Decorate the door hanger with foam stickers (optional).

4. Have the boys put the doorhanger in a place they will see it every day. Once they've completed their chores, move the clothes pin from the "To Do" side to the "Done" side.

Bazooka Boys ★ Who Am I?

THE WAY TO OBEY

WHAT'S THE POINT?
God wants us to obey, without delay, all the way, the right way!

THEME VERSE
Children, obey your parents the way the Lord wants, because this is the right thing to do.
Ephesians 6:1 (ERV)

RELATED BIBLE PASSAGE
Numbers 20:1–13

Have you ever played "Simon Says?" You know, the game where the leader tells you what to do and you have to do whatever they say? It's such a fun game to play, especially if you get to be the one telling everyone what to do. **OH, THE POWER!** Mwahhhhhhhhaaaa! (Insert evil laugh here.) It's fun to be in charge of other people!

It's super fun to be the leader in "Simon Says," and it's still kind of fun to be the one following directions. But it isn't always fun to have to do what other people tell you to do in real life. Like when your mom tells you to do your homework before playing with your friends (ugh!). Or when your teacher tells you to stop talking to your neighbor and finish your assignment (double ugh!). Or when your dad tells you to organize the garage while your friends are all going to the movies (triple super-duper ugh!).

God puts people in our lives who are kind of the boss of us while we're young. Romans 13:1 says, "*For all authority comes from God, and those in positions of authority have been placed there by God*" (NLT). These people have been put in authority by God to take care of us and help us grow. They keep us safe and teach us how to become good, responsible people. These people are your parents, teachers, leaders, pastors, coaches, and others in positions of authority over you. God wants us to honor them in many ways, including speaking respectfully, listening to what they say, and most importantly, obeying them.

"FOR ALL AUTHORITY COMES FROM GOD, AND THOSE IN POSITIONS OF AUTHORITY HAVE BEEN PLACED THERE BY GOD." (NLT)

OBEY—that's kind of a funny word, isn't it? Do you know what it means? It means to do whatever someone in authority over you tells you to do. It means to follow their instructions or commands. It means listening to directions and following those directions.

It's very important to remember that, first and foremost, God wants us to obey Him. He has given us instructions in the Bible, and it matters a lot to Him that we obey those instructions. Jeremiah 42:6 says, *"Whether we like it or not, we will obey the Lord our God to whom we are sending you with our plea. For if we obey him, everything will turn out well for us"*. Sometimes we may not want to do the right thing, but this verse reminds us that when we choose to do the things God has told us to do (and when we choose **NOT** to do the things God has told us **NOT** to do), things will go well for us. If we choose to disobey God, we're going to have some problems and things will not go well for us. But if we follow His instructions, He has promised to lead us on the best possible path for our lives!

God wants us to obey Him, and He wants us to obey the authority figures He has put in our lives. Ephesians 6:1 tells us, *"Children, obey your parents the way the Lord wants, because this is the right thing to do"* (ERV). Obeying your parents, teachers, and leaders is an important part of growing up and honoring God with your life.

THAT'S NOT ALWAYS EASY, IS IT?

Sometimes we just don't feel like doing what we've been told to do. Sometimes we don't like the instructions we've been given. Sometimes we're just lazy or want to do things our own way. Obedience might seem like a simple idea, but it's certainly not easy!

If we want to honor God, we need to learn to obey. So here are three ways we can honor God with our obedience.

The first way, is to...

 # 1. OBEY WITHOUT DELAY.

When Dalton got home from school one day, he was exhausted. He dropped his coat and backpack on the floor in the hallway and ran to the kitchen to grab a granola bar and juice box. His mom yelled down the stairs, "Dalton! Make sure you hang up your coat and backpack!"

Dalton yelled back, "Okay," but he was digging through the box for his favorite flavor of juice box and was distracted by all the yumminess. Once he found just the right beverage, he remembered he wanted to check his iPad to see if there was a message from his friend about meeting at the park, so he ran to the desk when he heard his mom yell down the stairs again, "Dalton, did you hang up your coat and backpack?" He yelled back, "Just a minute!" as he scrolled through his messages looking for a reply. He really intended to go hang up his backpack just as soon as he replied to his friend, but he remembered that he was in the middle of a super awesome game and was **JUST** about to finish a level, so he sat down and started playing.

A few minutes later, he looked up to see his mom standing in front of him with a not-so-happy look on her face. "Dalton! I told you to pick up your coat and backpack!" Dalton, suddenly remembered what he was supposed to do and felt bad that he hadn't obeyed his mother right away. He meant to do it, but he got distracted and ended up disobeying what his mother had said to do.

When our parents, teachers, or coaches ask us to do something, we need to obey **RIGHT THEN**. It's not okay to say, "I'll eventually get to it," or "I'll do it later!" That is not obeying. It's also not okay to ignore someone when they're giving you instructions or put off doing the thing they tell you to do. Being obedient means immediately doing the thing being asked of us, not waiting until later,

Bazooka Boys ★ Who Am I?

not getting around to it eventually, not ignoring instructions. It means obeying without delay.

Most importantly, it's important to quickly obey God when He tells you to do something. Psalm 119:60 says, *"I won't waste any time. I will be quick to obey your commands"* (NIRV). Obeying God and others immediately is the only way to obey.

The second way we can honor God with our obedience is to…

 ## 2. OBEY ALL THE WAY.

Have your parents ever told you to clean up your room? Then when you walk in, you realize what a total disaster it is and instead of actually picking up the toys and clothes, you simply shove everything into the closet or under the bed? Is that really obeying what your parents have told you to do? I don't think so.

Obeying means you do what has been asked of you completely. You do exactly what you have been told to do, and you do a good job. Doing something half way isn't obedience.

There's a story in the Bible that shows how God feels about half-way obedience. Moses led the Israelites out of Egypt, and now they were wandering around in the wilderness. It was hot, and they were thirsty! Moses and his brother Aaron prayed and asked God to miraculously provide something for the people to drink. God told Moses to speak to a rock, and then water would flow out of it. (Umm…super cool!)

When Moses got to the rock, he didn't follow God's instructions. He was frustrated with the people and all their grumbling and complaining. Instead of speaking to the rock like God told him to, he hit it with his staff instead. Now, God didn't want to see His people die of thirst, so He caused water to come out of the rock anyway.

But God was not very happy with Moses and Aaron. Numbers 20:12 says, "*God said to Moses and Aaron, 'Because you didn't trust me, didn't treat me with holy reverence in front of the People of Israel, you two aren't going to lead this company into the land that I am giving them.'*" God punished them for not doing exactly what He had told them to do. Not only did they strike the rock instead of speaking to it, they didn't remind the people that the miracle came from God, and they took the glory of the miracle for themselves. Because of their disobedience, they were not able to enter the Promised Land. They were punished because they didn't obey God all the way.

When God asks you to do something, do it until it's complete. When your parents tell you something, follow their instructions. When your teachers or coaches give you directions, do your very best to do what they say. Don't do things halfway—obey all the way.

The last way we can honor God with our obedience is to…

 ## 3. OBEY tHE RIGHt WAY.

All of us have been asked to do things that we **REALLY** don't want to do. We already talked about the idea that God wants us to obey, all the way, without delay. It's also important to obey with a good attitude and good effort.

Sometimes that can be really hard! Maybe your mom told you to clean your room and you obeyed her, but the whole time you were cleaning you stomped your feet and slammed doors. Or maybe you complained and whined the whole time. Or maybe you did the job as slow as possible just because you were trying to make sure everyone knew how **UNHAPPY** you were that you had to clean your room.

Do you think obeying with a bad attitude is pleasing to God? I don't think so. Of course it's important to follow through even when you don't feel like it, but it's also important to obey with the right heart and actions.

Bazooka Boys ★ Who Am I?

Philippians 2:14 says, *"Do everything without complaining or arguing"* (NIRV). We need to check our attitude while we're obeying. Are we "technically" obeying while throwing a fit? Or, are we working with a good attitude even if it's not our favorite thing to do? God honors a good attitude because it's a sign of respect to those He has put in charge of us.

One last thought about obeying: God wants you to obey your earthly authority, but He wants you to obey His Word first and foremost. If you ever have an authority in your life wanting you to do or say something that goes against God's laws, you need to talk to a trusted adult about the situation. Sometimes adults make mistakes too, and God doesn't want you doing things you know are wrong because you're trying to obey someone who's leading you down the wrong path. Talk to someone you trust, and they'll help you figure out the best way to handle your situation.

Obeying God is more important than anything else in your life. When you listen carefully to the things He tells you to do, doing your very best to do them quickly, thoroughly, and with a good attitude, things will go well for you!

ACTIVITY SHEET

In the squares write:
Complain, whine, cry, yell, stomp

In the circles write:
Ignore, delay, wait, disobey

In the hearts write:
Obey, without, all, right

Color all the circles green.

Color all the squares blue.

Color all the hearts red.

Now fill in the blanks with the words in the hearts:

God wants us to _____ , _____ delay,

_____ the way, the _____ way!

When we obey God, we do what He tells us to. We follow the path He wants us to take instead of choosing our own way. Complete the maze below and remind yourself to choose God's path!

Bazooka Boys ★ Who Am I?

Look up the following verses in your Bible and underline them with a color pencil. Then write them out in the space provided. Write out one way you can follow the truth in your own life in the heart next to each verse.

Ephesians 6:1

Jeremiah 42:6

Psalm 119:60

Do you remember what we learned today? Fill in the blanks.

God wants us to _____ , _____ delay,

_____ the way, the _____ way!

Word List:
right   *obey*   *delay*   *without*

ACTIVITY SHEET

START ↓

FINISH! ↑

Bazooka Boys ★ Who Am I?

BAZOOKA BREAKDOWN

God wants us to obey without delay. Think of an example of a time when you didn't obey right away. Draw a picture of yourself in that situation.

When we're asked to do something by someone in authority over us, is it okay to only obey part of their instructions? Check the box with the right answer.

We need to obey with a good attitude. Think of a time when you did something you weren't really excited about, but you did it with a good attitude anyway. Write 4 words to describe your attitude and write them in the boxes below.

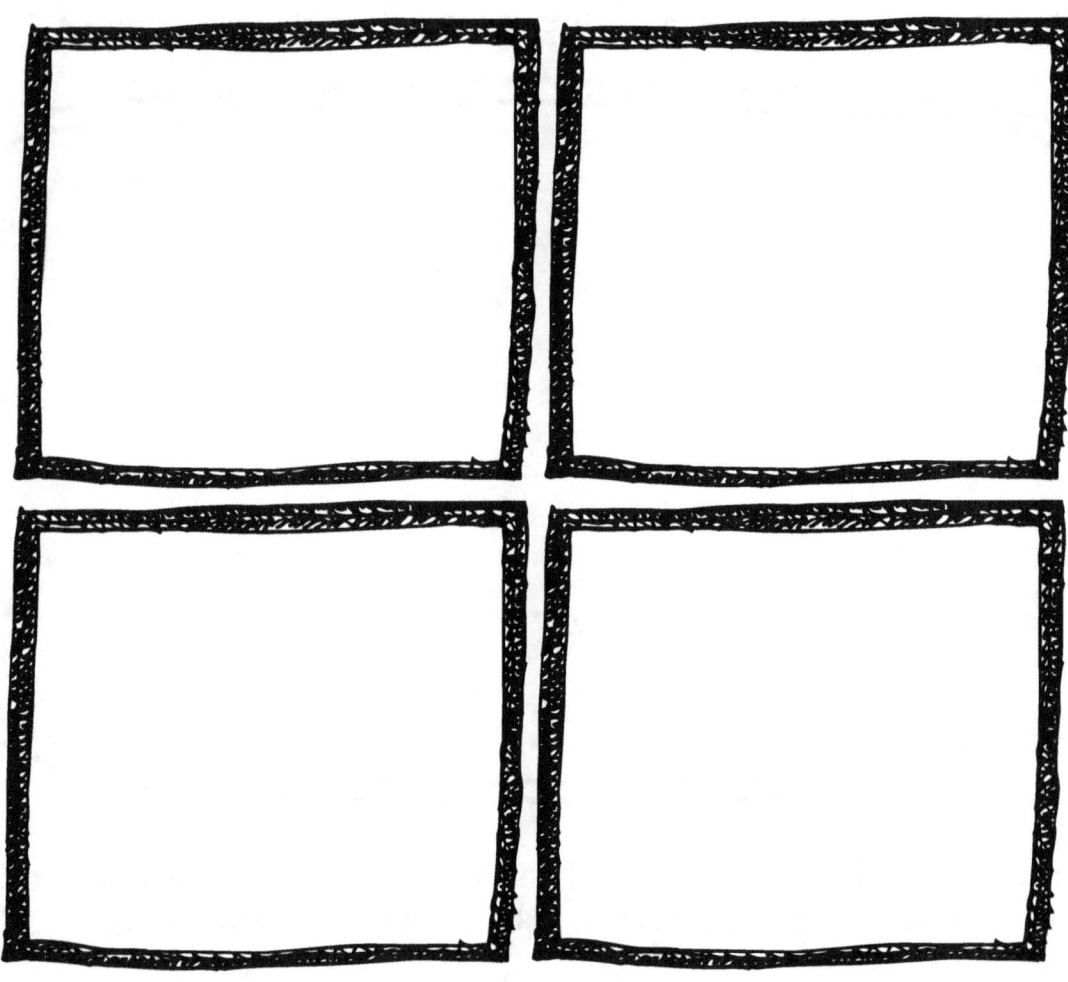

Bazooka Boys ★ Who Am I?

"DO WHAT I SAY" MAZE CHALLENGE

Try this fun project with a friend!

<u>Supplies</u>

- Maze templates
- Blindfolds
- Markers or crayons

<u>Prep</u>

- Copy maze template onto paper (1 of each level of difficulty per boy).

<u>Directions</u>

1. One boy will be blindfolded, and the other will give directions.

2. When you say "go" the blindfolded boy must follow the instructions of his partner to lead him through the maze.

3. When one boy has completed the maze, they should switch roles.

4. Each boy should take turns with the more challenging mazes until everyone has completed each round.

5. Think about how important it was to listen and obey the directions of your partner!

YOUR BODY, GOD'S HOUSE

WHAT'S THE POINT?
Our bodies are God's house, and we need to take good care of His house!

THEME VERSE
You know that you are God's house. The spirit of God lives in you.
1 Corinthians 3:16 (WE)

RELATED BIBLE PASSAGE
Daniel 1:8–19

What does your house look like? Do you have your own room, or do you share with someone? Did you get to decorate your room a certain way? The place where we live is a very special—it's where we spend time with our family, where we come to rest and relax, where we get away from all the craziness of the world. It's the special place that belongs to us and the people we love.

I don't know about you, but there's nothing I love more than coming home after a long, busy day and walking into my house, where I can smell yummy things cooking and see all the things and people I love. Our homes are important!

Did you know God has a house? It's true—He does! It might surprise you to learn where God's house is. It's not a church or a big mansion. It's actually **YOU**! The Bible tells us the spirit of God lives inside of us in 1 Corinthians 3:16: *"You know that you are God's house. The spirit of God lives in you"* (WE). When we ask Jesus to come into our life, He makes His home inside of us. He lives in us and helps us in every way possible. What a cool thought!

Since God's house is inside our bodies, don't you think it's important for us to take care of our bodies? What would happen to your real house if you never took care of it, if you never took out the trash or cleaned up the dishes? What if you never painted the outside or made sure the grass was mowed? It wouldn't take long before your house would be broken down, messed up, and not very much fun to live in.

Just like we take care of our physical houses, we need to take care of our bodies—God's house!

Bazooka Boys ★ Who Am I?

What are some ways you can take good care of God's house?

 # 1. TAKE GOOD CARE OF YOUR BODY.

Sam was so excited to **FINALLY** be on summer vacation—no more getting up early to catch the bus, no more homework, no more school lunches! He couldn't wait to just lie around and relax.

He started staying up **WAY** too late every night. He would sneak a flashlight into his room and read his book well into the night. Then he'd sleep in late and stumble down into the kitchen and pour himself a bowl of super-sugary cereal and eat a couple doughnuts. Then he laid on the couch, watching TV for the rest of the morning. He forgot to brush his teeth and decided he'd get to it later. He even forgot to take a shower like his mom told him to do.

By the time dinner rolled around, Sam wasn't feeling so great. His body was **NOT** happy with him. His muscles ached, his tummy hurt, and he felt pretty blah. He realized that, although it sounds fun to be lazy and eat junk all day long, it really made him feel horrible! He decided to go to bed early and try to do better the next day.

God wants you to take good care of your body! That means eating healthy foods, getting plenty of exercise, brushing your teeth every day, and taking baths or showers to make sure that your body stays clean. Taking care of God's house means taking good care of your body!

The second way you can take good care of your bodies is to...

 # 2. PUT GOOD THINGS INTO YOUR BODY.

Have you ever watched your mom or dad put gas in the car? The gas is the fuel that makes the car work! Your body works the same way—what you put inside it determines how well your body works. Your food is supposed to give your body power.

There are two kinds of food we can put into our bodies: lazy foods and power foods. Lazy foods are full of sugar and fat. They might taste good, but they don't give us any power. Lazy foods include sugary cereals, candy, fast food, and other greasy things.

Power foods fill our bodies with good things that build up our muscles and give us energy. They're filled with vitamins and minerals and protein that give our bodies the fuel they need to work hard. Power foods make your body healthy and strong! Some yummy power foods are fruits, vegetables, nuts, whole grains and lean meat.

When you're choosing the foods you put in your body, choose power foods over lazy foods. Your body will thank you!

The last way you can take good care of your bodies is to…

3. PRACTICE SELF-CONTROL WHEN YOU MAKE YOUR FOOD CHOICES.

I know it seems like a really good idea to eat ten cookies for breakfast, but is that really a good choice? Sometimes we open a bag of candy and just can't seem to help ourselves from eating every last piece right before dinner. It's just so yummy!

One of the biggest areas where we need to practice self-control throughout our lives is what we eat. Your tummy might be screaming loudly, "EAT MORE SUGAR! GIVE ME MORE DONUTS! DON't EAT THOSE VEGETABLES! GIVE ME POTATO CHIPS INSTEAD!" In that moment, you have to use your self-control to make a better choice to eat things that make your body healthy.

Here's a fun way to help yourself practice self-control with your food—try using the "Go-Slow-Whoa" trick when choosing your food.

Bazooka Boys ★ Who Am I?

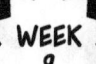

GO foods are the very best **POWER** foods—foods that are always a good idea: fruits, veggies, water, and healthy protein like lean meats, yogurt, and nuts. Choose **GO** foods for most of your daily meals and snacks. Your body will be full of power and energy when you give it this kind of food.

SLOW foods are foods that are good to eat sometimes. They're not really bad for you, but you should only eat them occasionally. They're higher in fat and sugar and have more calories. **SLOW** foods include breads and pastas, cheese, and processed foods. Slow foods still have some nutrition in them, but your diet shouldn't only include **SLOW** foods.

And then there are **WHOA** foods. These are for special occasions. They're high in sugar and fat and don't have much nutritional value. It's okay to have cake or ice cream every once in a while, but if you eat too much too often, your body won't have any energy. If your diet is full of **WHOA** foods, your body won't be working as well as it should be.

Remember, your body is God's house. He made our bodies, and He wants us to take good care of them! Psalm 100:3 says, *"Know that the Lord is God. He made us, and we belong to Him."* When we remember that our bodies belong to God, we'll want to make sure they're as strong and healthy as they can be. This is a great way to show God you're glad He lives inside of you.

DOODLE PAGE

LESSON 9

Draw a picture of **THREE LAZY FOODS** which don't give you energy!

Draw a picture of **THREE POWER FOODS** which make you strong!

ACTIVITY SHEET

WEEK 9

The Bible says our bodies are God's house. Each one of us has a body that is unique, just the way God made us. Color and decorate this house with your favorite colors and shapes. Make it special, just like you!

We show God we love Him by taking care of the bodies He has given us. Circle the pictures of things that are healthy for our bodies.

Bazooka Boys ★ Who Am I?

Solve the puzzle below to remind yourself where God lives.

1 Corinthians 3:16 (WE)

A	B	C	D	E	F	G	H	I	J	K	L	M	N	O	P	R	S	T	U	V	W	Y
19	9	12	5	21	20	1	17	25	4	3	2	13	16	18	8	10	11	7	14	6	26	22

Y O U — K N O W — T H A T — Y O U
22 18 14 — 3 16 18 26 — 7 17 19 7 — 22 18 14

A R E — G O D ' S — H O U S E .
19 10 21 — 1 18 5 — 11 — 17 18 14 11 21

T H E — S P I R I T — O F — G O D
7 17 21 — 11 8 25 10 25 7 — 18 20 — 1 18 5

L I V E S — I N — Y O U .
2 25 6 21 11 — 25 16 — 22 18 14

We can make healthy choices when it comes to the food we put into our bodies. In the space below, list some things that are **GO** foods, **SLOW** foods, and **WHOA** foods.

GO	SLOW	WHOA

As we get older, we can sometimes feel bad about how our bodies feel different. It's important to remind yourself that God created your body unique and different on purpose. He wants your body to be healthy, but that doesn't mean every body will look the same. Look up Psalm 139:14 and write it out in the space provided. Then make a list of the ways God made your body unique (things like hair color, eye color, skin color, and any other thing that makes you YOU).

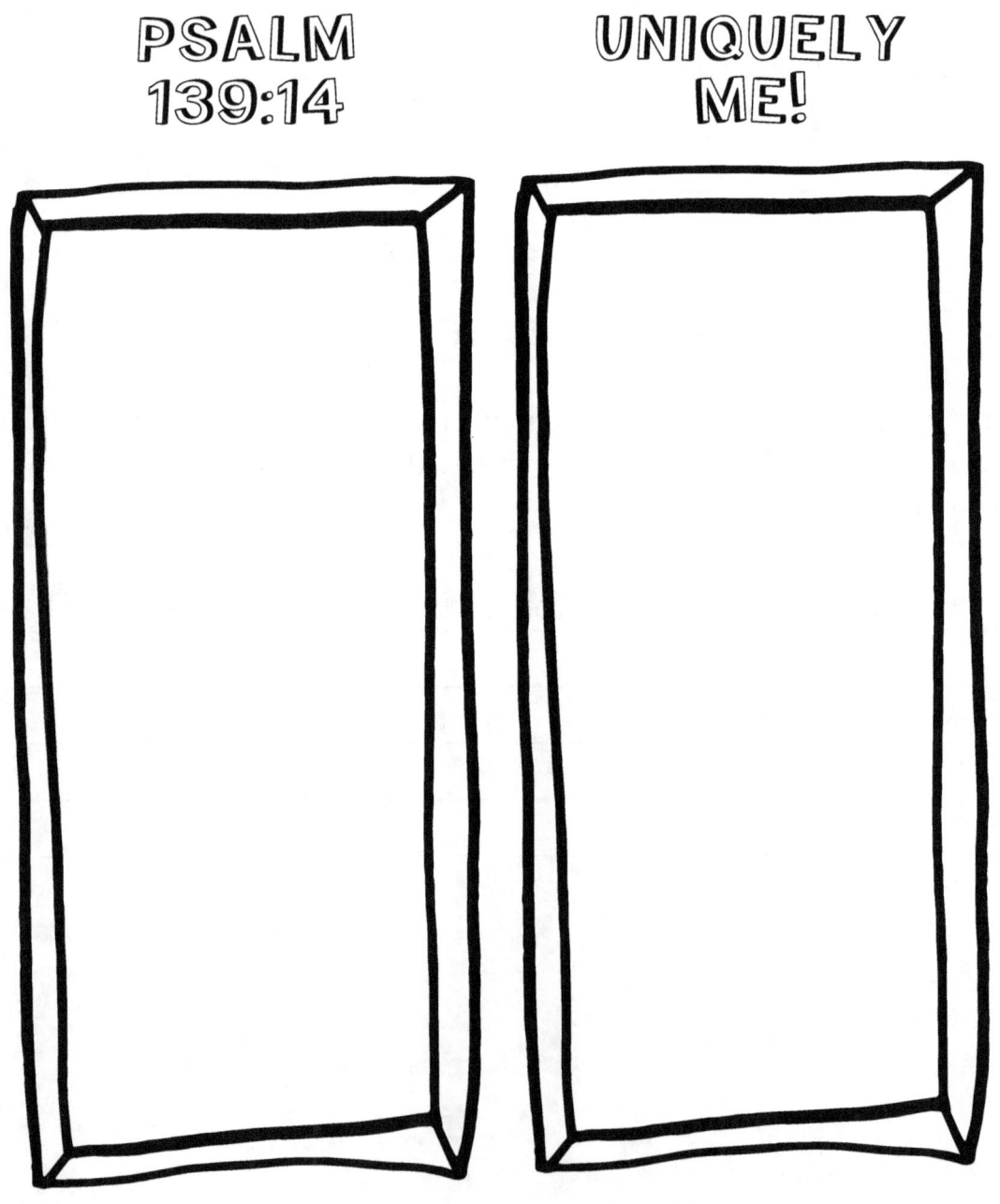

Bazooka Boys ★ Who Am I?

What are some ways you can take good care of your body? Write your 5 best answers in the space below.

_____

_____

_____

_____

_____

We talked about three different kinds of foods. Write out your favorite from each group in the space below.

GO! _____

SLOW! _____

WHOA! _____

What is one thing can you do this week to make better food choices?

MONSTER CHOMP

Supplies

- Plastic Cup
- White paper
- Pencil
- String
- Tape
- Glue stick
- Broccoli floret

Prep

- Tie a broccoli floret to a string cut about 18" long

Directions

1. Trace the open side of the cup onto the paper making a circle.
2. Draw a line through the center of the circle.
3. Draw a zig zag over the center line to create "monster teeth."
4. Cut along the zig zag to create two halves.
5. Glue halves to the rim of the cup, one on top and one on bottom.
6. Tape the string to the inside bottom of the cup with the piece of broccoli hanging down. (Or poke a hole and tie a knot on the outside of the cup)
7. Try to get your monster to eat his broccoli by swinging it and catching it in his mouth.

Bazooka Boys ★ Who Am I?

HANDS AND FEET

What's the Point?
Our bodies belong to God and we need to use them the way He wants us to!

THEME VERSE
But I discipline my body and keep it under control.
1 Corinthians 9:27

RELATED BIBLE PASSAGE
Romans 6:12–14

Last week we talked about the fact that our bodies are God's house. The Bible says He lives inside of us, so we need to take good care of His house. We should be taking good care of our bodies by exercising, eating good foods, and making sure we stay clean and healthy.

Today we're going to talk more about practicing self-control with our bodies. We need to make sure every part of us is behaving in a way that shows others we belong to God.

Can you think of a time when it seemed like your body was in control of you? Maybe you could **NOT** stay awake during class or church. No matter how hard you tried, your eyes would **NOT** stay open. Your body wanted to sleep, and it seemed like nothing you did kept you awake!

Or maybe you were **REALLY** hungry and your stomach kept growling and growling. No matter how hard you tried **NOT** to, all you could think about was a double cheeseburger with extra bacon and cheese, and your stomach got louder and louder until everyone could hear it.

Or maybe you had to go to the bathroom really, really bad and you just kept jumping and dancing around thinking, "I can wait! I'm having so much fun with my friends. I don't want to stop playing to go inside." Pretty soon you realize that you better go **NOW** because your body is going to take over and you're going to go to the bathroom whether or not you're **IN** the bathroom.

Bazooka Boys ★ Who Am I?

Our bodies can sure be bossy. Sometimes we find ourselves in a situation where we do something with our bodies that we know isn't right. If we wanted to, we could stop ourselves, but we just don't practice self-control.

Have you ever done something with your hands that hurt another person? Maybe you hit your little sister or took something from your neighbor that didn't belong to you. Maybe you wrote something mean about another person or pushed someone because they made you mad.

Have you ever let your feet take you into a situation that you knew wasn't good? Maybe you went over to a friend's house even though you knew your mom had told you not to. Maybe you ran away from a friend who wanted to play with you and hurt his feelings by excluding him. Maybe you stomped your feet in a temper tantrum because you didn't get your way. Or maybe you kicked the door to your bedroom when your mom grounded you for having a bad attitude.

Proverbs 6:18 tells us that God **HATES** *"feet that are quick to do wrong."* Does that mean that God doesn't like feet? Of course not! It means God doesn't like it when we let our feet take us places that will get us into trouble.

We need to keep our bodies under control. God wants our hands and feet to do good things for Him, not things that could hurt other people or disobey our parents.

What are some things you can do to practice self-control with your body?

You need to...

 1. THINK BEFORE YOU ACT.

Sometimes we do things with our bodies before we stop to think about our actions. Have you ever heard the word "impulsive"? It means you do something before you stop and think.

Instead of reacting in the moment when you're mad or sad or angry, try stopping yourself **BEFORE** you act. Take a deep breath and count to three. Then think about your actions and possible consequences. Are you going to hurt someone?

Are you going to make someone sad? Think about how **YOU** would feel if the same thing was done to you, **THEN** make a good choice regarding your actions.

Another smart idea is to ask yourself a few questions before you act. What will happen if you do the thing you're thinking about doing? What will happen if you **DON'T** do the thing you're thinking about doing? Look at both choices and decide which is the better option.

Ephesians 5:17 says, "*Don't act thoughtlessly, but understand what the Lord wants you to do.*" When you act before you think, you're acting thoughtlessly. Stop yourself before you act and ask God if this action will be pleasing to Him. Then make the choice to honor God with your actions.

I know it can be **REALLY** hard to stop yourself when you want to react to something, but it can take just **SECONDS** to say or do something that will have lasting effects on you and others. Don't let your actions happen before you have a chance to think about them. Stop and think. Then act.

The second way we can have self-control with our bodies is to...

 ## 2. RESPECT OTHER PEOPLE'S BODIES.

God gave each one of us a body, and He cares about us! He wants us to care about other people, too. When you do something that hurts or bothers another person, that isn't pleasing to God.

There was a boy in Avery's class who always bothered him. He kicked his chair in class and untied his shoes at recess. Sometimes he would try to distract Avery by making funny noises during quizzes. One day he pushed him down on the playground and he finally had enough.

"You better stop this right now!" he yelled loudly. "You are always in my personal space, and if you don't stop it right now, I'm going to talk to the teacher and make sure you get into trouble." The boy walked away laughing, but Avery felt good that he had stood up for himself.

YOUR BODY BELONGS TO YOU. NO ONE ELSE SHOULD BOTHER YOU, HURT YOU, OR DO THINGS THAT MAKE YOU FEEL UNCOMFORTABLE.

In the same way, you should always respect other people's bodies. Be kind and careful when you're playing games. Don't push or shove others. Don't distract others by poking them, throwing things, or doing anything else that could keep them from doing their best when they're trying to concentrate.

Philippians 2:3 says, *"In whatever you do, don't let selfishness or pride be your guide. Be humble, and honor others more than yourselves"* (ERV). God wants you to care about other people, and that includes respecting their bodies.

The last way you can practice self-control with your body is to…

 ## 3. KEEP YOUR BODY UNDER CONTROL.

It's not easy to keep your body under control, but that is exactly what you need to do every single day. First Corinthians 9:27 says, *"But I discipline my body and keep it under control."* God wants us to be in charge of what our bodies do. This means practicing self-control instead of letting our bodies do whatever comes to mind.

You can practice self-control with your body when you choose NOT to hit someone when you get angry with them. You can practice self-control when you refuse to throw a tantrum even though you're disappointed that your parents won't let you do something. You can practice self-control when you respond to your sister with a calm, quiet voice instead of yelling at her. You can practice self-control with your body by sitting still when the teacher has asked you not to get up from your desk. None of these things are easy, but you can do them! God has promised to help you practice self-control. If you pray and ask God for His help, He has promised to give you the strength to be disciplined with your actions.

ACTIVITY SHEET

WEEK 10

Write the word **BODY** in the blank spaces below.

But don't let sin control your life here on earth. You must not be ruled by the things your sinful self makes you want to do. Don't offer the parts of your _____ to serve sin. Don't use your _____ to do evil, but offer yourselves to God, as people who have died and now live. Offer the parts of your _____ to God to be used for doing good. – Romans 6:12–13 (ERV)

Today we learned that we should think before we act. In the scenarios below, circle the **RIGHT** way to act in each situation.

1. Someone takes your toy:

    a. Hitting back   b. Asking for toy back

2. Your sister is being annoying:

    a. Kick your sister   b. Walk away

3. You don't get the candy you want at the store:

    a. Throw a tantrum   b. Be sad but accept it

4. You lose at softball:

    a. Cry "It's not fair, you cheated!"   b. Shake hands with other team and say "Good job"

We need to respect other people's bodies and personal space. Philippians 2:3 says, "*In whatever you do, don't let selfishness or pride be your guide. Be humble, and honor others more than yourselves*" (ERV).

Find the hidden words below.

R	I	H	X	E	A	R	E
V	P	O	C	N	T	M	L
D	G	M	X	E	M	O	B
S	D	H	D	Y	K	P	M
G	Z	I	M	A	L	O	U
X	R	H	O	N	O	R	H
P	S	V	H	F	H	P	L
H	P	M	X	E	S	D	G

Word List:

Humble

Honor

Pride

Bazooka Boys ★ Who Am I?

WEEK 10

Some key words are missing in the verse below. Using the first letter of the word as a clue, fill in the missing words using the key below.

But don't let sin C_____ your life here on earth. You must not be ruled by the things your S_____ self makes you want to do. Don't offer the parts of your B_____ to serve sin. Don't use your B_____ to do evil, but offer Y_____ to God, as people who have died and now live. Offer the parts of your B_____ to God to be used for doing G_____.

– Romans 6:12–13 (ERV)

Word List

Good	*Yourselves*	*Sinful*
Body	*Control*	

Today we learned that we should think before we act. In the scenarios below, circle the **RIGHT** way to act in each situation.

1. Someone takes your toy:
    a. Hitting back   b. Asking for toy back

2. Your sister is being annoying:
    a. Kick your sister   b. Walk away

3. You don't get the candy you want at the store:
    a. Throw a tantrum   b. Be sad but accept it

4. You lose at softball:
    a. Cry "It's not fair, you cheated!"   b. Shake hands with other team and say "Good job"

Today we learned we need to think before we act. For each scenario below, write out the wrong way to react and the right way to act.

1. Someone steals your spot in line.

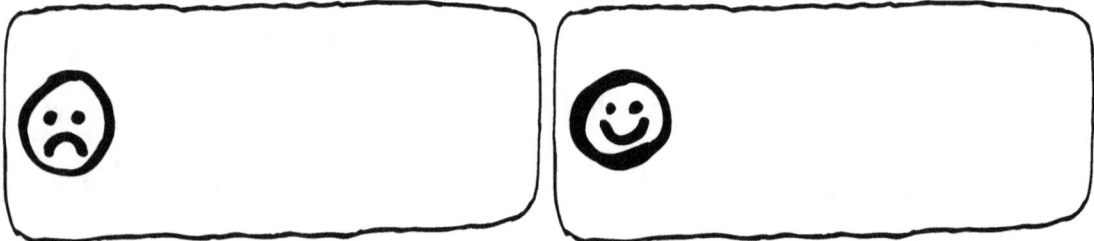

2. Your sister is driving you crazy and you just want her to leave you alone.

3. Your friend didn't invite you to her party and your feelings are hurt.

4. You lose the championship game and you're really upset.

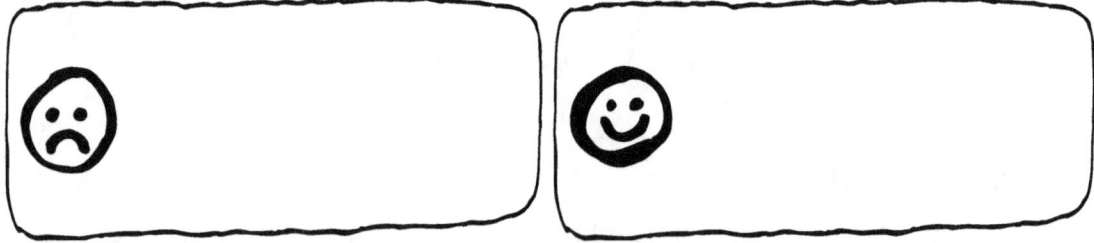

5. Your brother takes the last Fruit Roll-Up and he KNEW you wanted it.

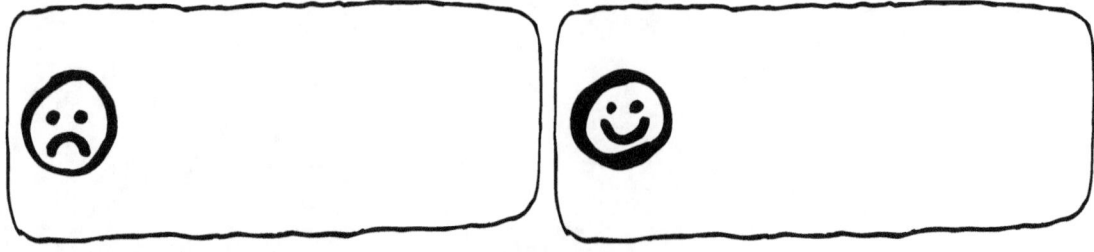

Bazooka Boys ★ Who Am I?

WEEK 10

We need to respect other people's bodies and personal space. Philippians 2:3 says, *"In whatever you do, don't let selfishness or pride be your guide. Be humble, and honor others more than yourselves"* (ERV).

Find the hidden words below.

```
I O V H R Q E P M W D C D Q O
P Q I O Z O K T M T U K D G C
L E D I R P N N W B J R W B U
K C M I F G H O C P I U Z K A
R M N X N H V Z H H G D Z X X
Y L H A U E P X Z Q U C G H T
S E L M P C V E U F U Q P O R
U U B Q S A F G R H O O P I E
H L S E P P A C S R J Y U S
E H N Z P S F X M J O M X J P
A Q B H N R T Y O V Q N P D E
V T Z V J L J T T Z U L A Y C
X U S E L F I S H N E S S L T
E R I E M X O Z W P B Y X R L
D M C D N F K T H K M A W V J
```

Word List:

Honor   *Hoop*   *Hula*

Humble   *Personal*   *Pride*

Respect   *Selfishness* *Space*

153

BAZOOKA BREAKDOWN

If we're not careful, our bodies can hurt someone else. Think of some ways that we can hurt others with our hands and write them on the hand pictures below. Think of some ways we can hurt others with our feet and write them on the feet pictures.

Bazooka Boys ★ Who Am I?

WEEK 10

What are some ways you can respect other people's bodies by controlling your own body?

Write out the theme verse and see if you can memorize it!

"*But I discipline my body and keep it under control.*" —I Corinthians 9:27

Name one way you are going to keep your body under control this week. Write it on the stop sign!

Bazooka Boys ★ Who Am I?

STICKY HANDS

<u>Supplies</u>

- Sticky Hands toy (gel party favors with stretchy string)
- Index cards
- Tape
- Crayons/markers/colored pencils

<u>Prep</u>

- Purchase sticky hand toy
- Designate an area on the wall for the index cards to be posted.
- Make a tape line on the floor to stay behind.

<u>Directions</u>

1. Take four index cards and on each card, write an action (Two with actions that are good, and two that are bad.)

2. Tape the cards onto a wall.

3. Throw your sticky hands towards the cards on the wall.

4. If a hand sticks to a card, read it out loud. If it's a positive action, repost it to the wall. If it's a negative action, crumple it up and throw it away.

5. Keep throwing the hands until all the bad cards are in the trash.

Bazooka Boys ★ Who Am I?

www.ingramcontent.com/pod-product-compliance
Lightning Source LLC
Chambersburg PA
CBHW060423010526
44118CB00017B/2332